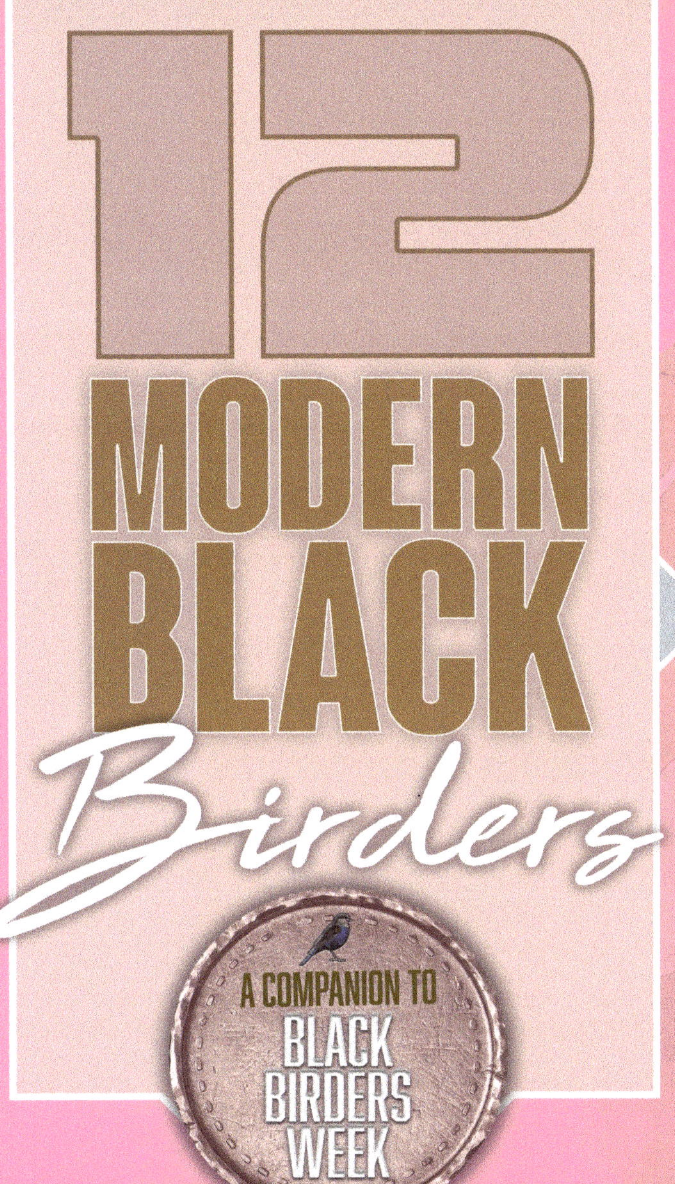

12 MODERN BLACK *Birders*

A COMPANION TO
BLACK BIRDERS WEEK

Layout and Design by Daniel J. Middleton

First published in the United States in May 2022 by Unique Coloring. Printed by Ingram Book Group, LLC.

ISBN: 978-1-935702-51-1 (Trade Paperback)

1 2 3 4 5 6 7 8 9 10   IBG   26 25 24 23 22

VISIT US ONLINE:
www.uniquecoloring.com

Biography Coloring

By **Daniel J. Middleton**

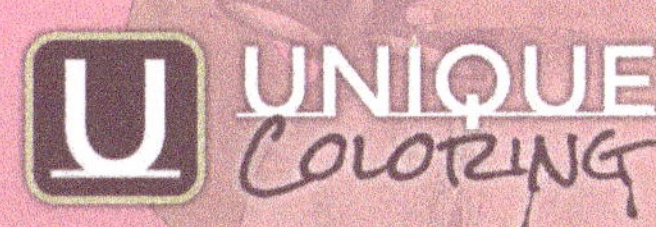

UNIQUE COLORING

INTRODUCTION

Welcome to Biography Coloring, where you will learn of a few interesting and noteworthy black birding enthusiasts and professionals while being able to color them! Read their stories to get familiar with their backgrounds before applying colors.

Some individuals featured in this book were instrumental in organizing Black Birders Week, which helped promote diversity outdoors since nature is for everyone. I am grateful to all the birders who agreed to interviews or corresponded via email to share photos and personal bios. In these pages, you will meet bird lovers and conservationists working in the field to protect various avian species.

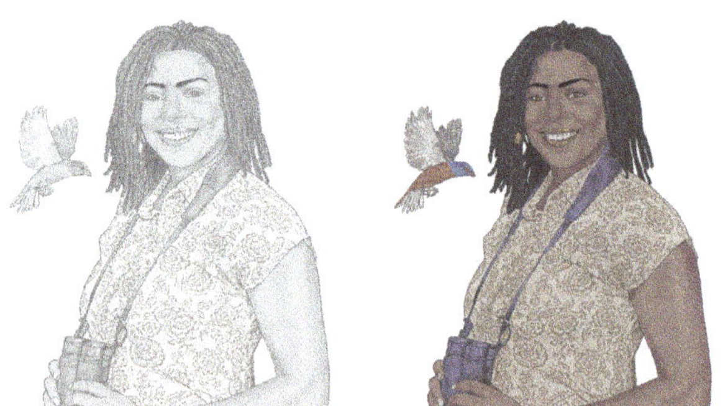

Grayscale page
pre-colored

Sample
colored page

Color each illustration using light mediums, such as premium colored pencils or quality crayons. If you prefer to use watercolors, pastels, markers, and heavier mediums, either apply a backing to the coloring pages before laying down color, or feel free to cut out the coloring pages and copy them to your paper of choice. Send me your finished artwork by taking digital photographs or scanning them. Then email me with the subject line 12 MODERN BLACK BIRDERS IN COLOR, and attach and send the artwork to the address below so it can be featured on the website:

uniquecoloring@gmail.com

With all of the preliminaries out of the way, I bid you happy reading and coloring!

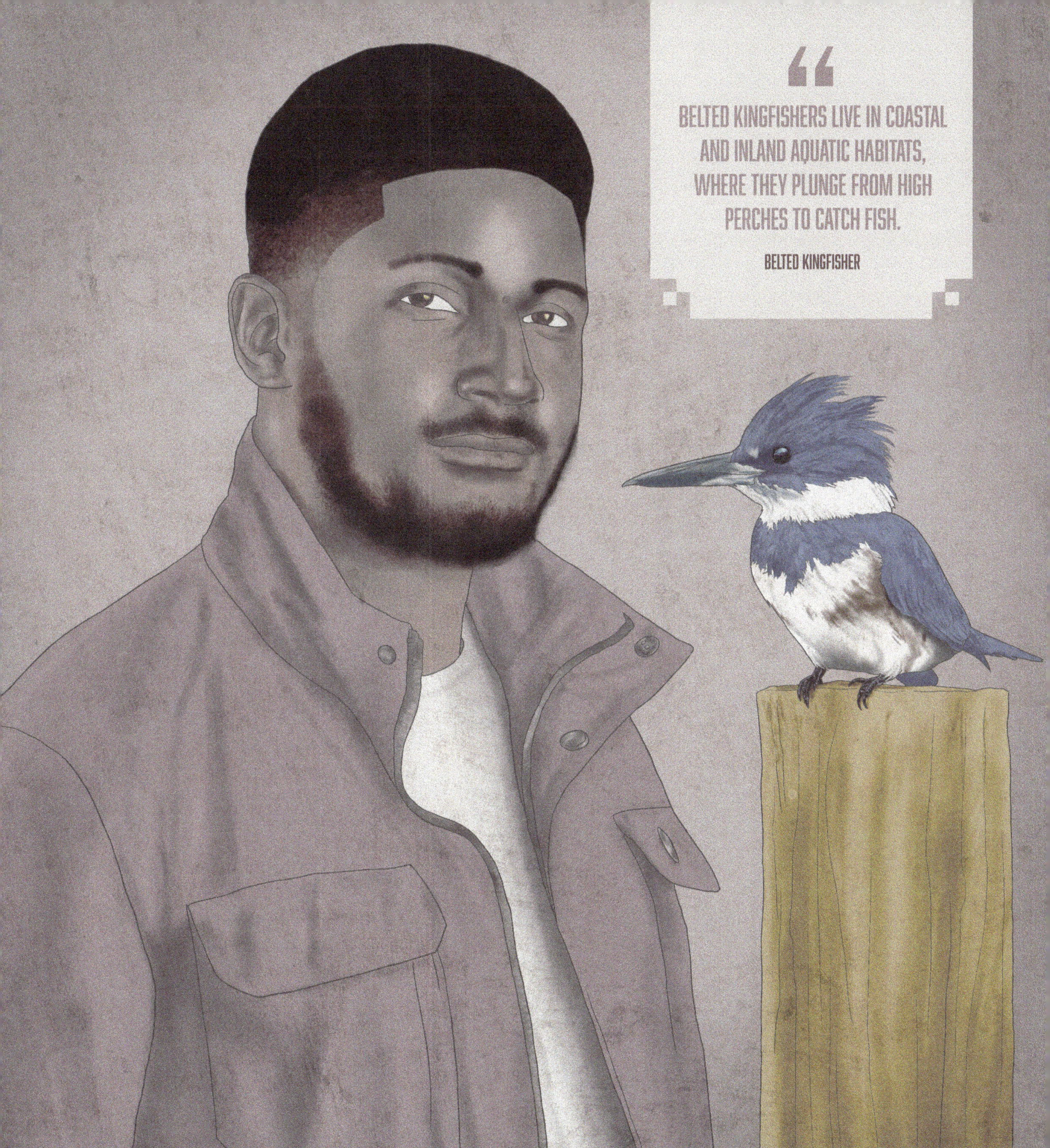
"
BELTED KINGFISHERS LIVE IN COASTAL
AND INLAND AQUATIC HABITATS,
WHERE THEY PLUNGE FROM HIGH
PERCHES TO CATCH FISH.
BELTED KINGFISHER

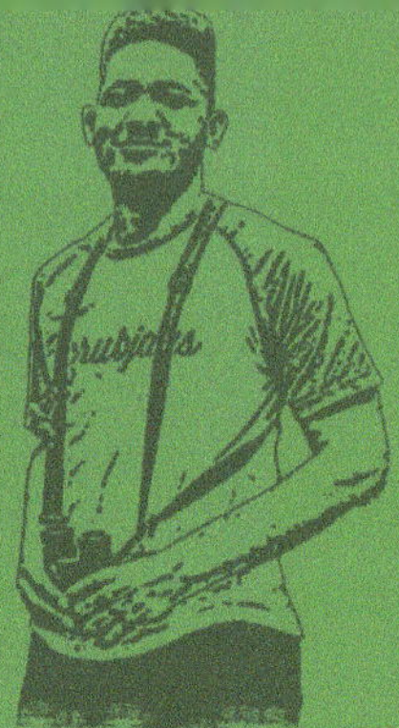

TYKEE JAMES

Tykee James is passionate about advocacy, be it in the realm of nature or human society.

As Government Affairs Coordinator for the National Audubon Society, he successfully merged those realms. That is evident in his various efforts, including an Audubon article he wrote for #BlackBirdersWeek in 2021. Tykee called for more inclusivity outdoors, where minorities would have access to green spaces sans racial discrimination. He also highlighted the need for more green spaces, as many new and seasoned bird watchers of color lack this infrastructure in their communities. Tykee cited two proposed federal bills aimed at facilitating these outcomes.

Tykee currently organizes bird walks for members of Congress and Congressional staff. Together with Jeffrey Train, he is co-founder of Freedom Birders, a project that seeks to decolonize birding and share the lessons of liberation through storytelling. But Freedom Birders is the arm of Amplify the Future, of which Tykee is co-chair and co-founder. The stated goal of the movement is to amplify "the future of STEAM and conservation by raising funds in support of historically excluded people with a connection to birds." Tykee also sits on the boards of directors of the D.C. Audubon Society, Wyncote Audubon Society, the Birding Co-op, Justice Outside, and the IDEAL Committee at the Academy of Natural Sciences at Drexel University.

Tykee James was born in Philadelphia, Pennsylvania, on January 21, 1994. Tykee had a natural curiosity as a child. He found joy in reading meteorology and astronomy books and watching National Geographic nature documentaries. But his family relocated a lot when he was young because his father was in the military. Tykee has three brothers. When he was three or four years old, the family moved to the west coast to live on a military base, Fort Irwin, situated midway between Los Angeles, California, and Las Vegas, Nevada, in what Tykee describes as "the middle of nowhere." A few years later, his parents divorced. Tykee and his brothers then lived with their mom in Racine, Wisconsin.

He later lived in two cities in Texas before moving back to Philadelphia, where he completed high school. Four and a half years at Temple University followed. Tykee landed his first job in Philly as an environmental educator. But despite that and his early interest in nature, a career in environmental conservation was not yet a focus. Instead, he entered politics. The local state representative, Donna Bullock—who Tykee supported—needed someone to run her schedule. She found Tykee on Facebook and saw that he was an environmental educator. Bullock reached out to him and asked if he would like to advise her on environmental policy. That was his entrance into the world of environmental advocacy. Suddenly, Tykee found his calling.

"Things pick up as far as speed because it happens pretty quickly. I worked in state representative Bullock's office from the start of 2015. And then my last day was sometime in November 2018, before I started my job at the National Audubon Society, December 3, 2018. Those three years were very formative." U

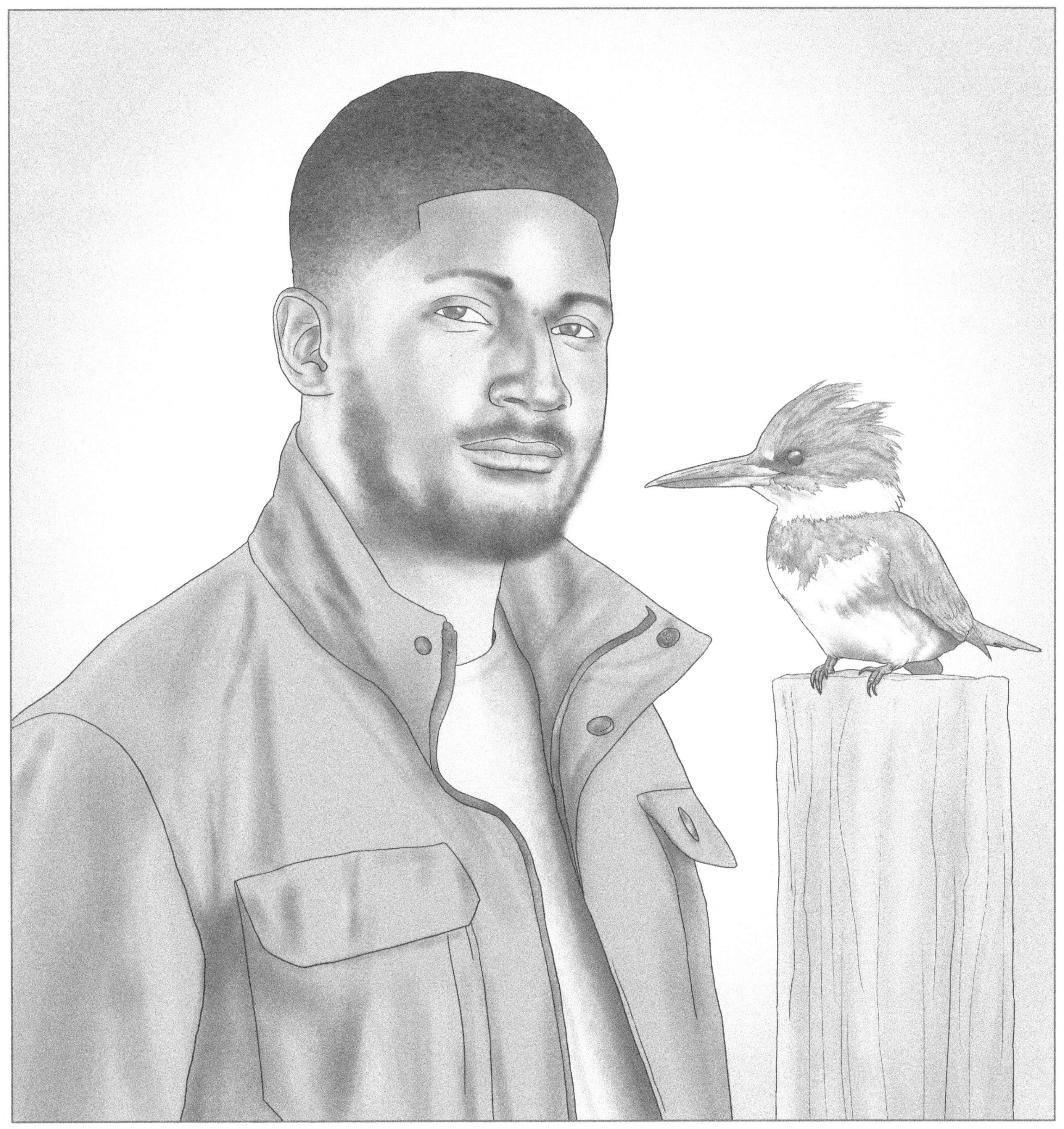

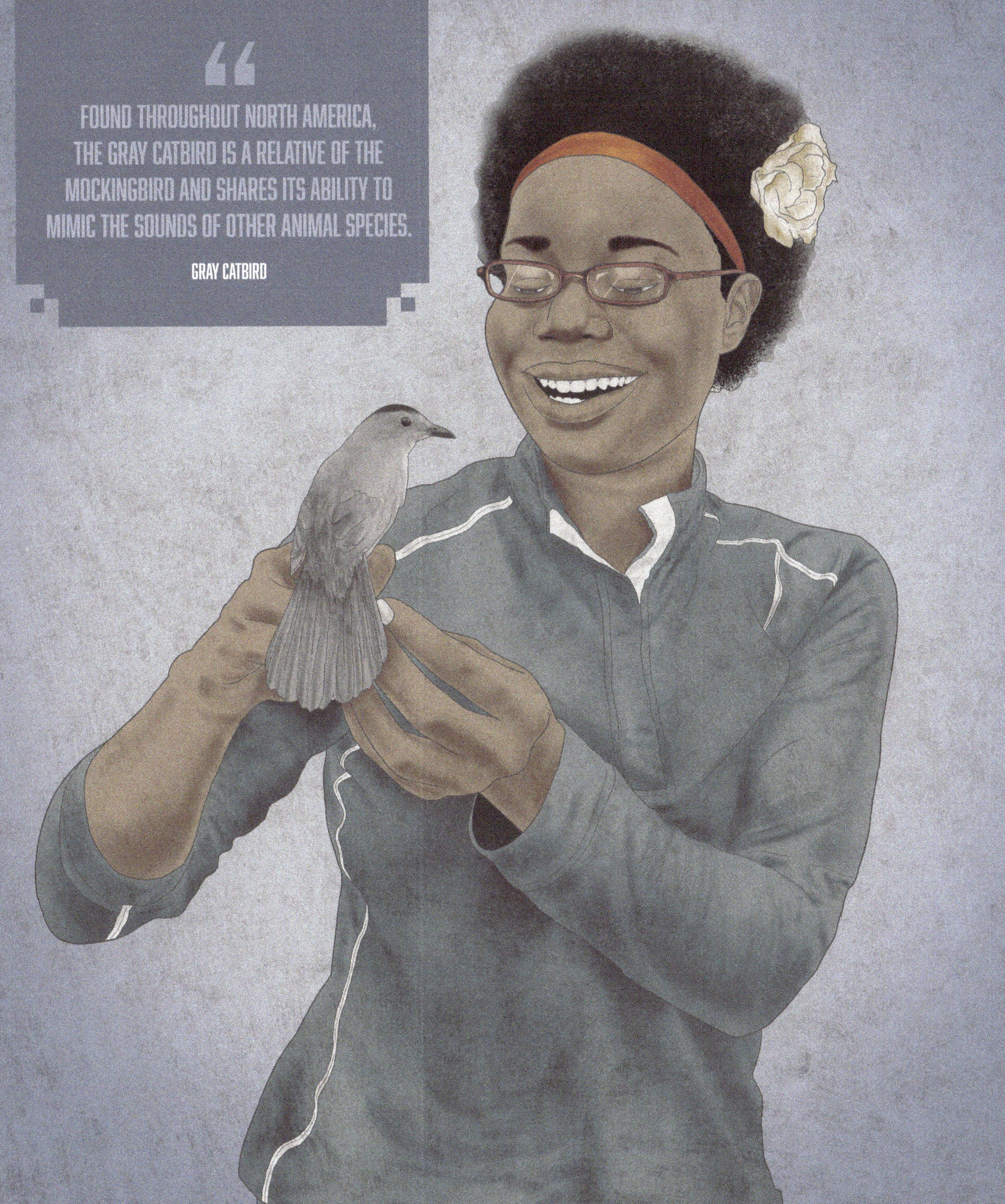

FOUND THROUGHOUT NORTH AMERICA,
THE GRAY CATBIRD IS A RELATIVE OF THE
MOCKINGBIRD AND SHARES ITS ABILITY TO
MIMIC THE SOUNDS OF OTHER ANIMAL SPECIES.

GRAY CATBIRD

NICOLE JACKSON

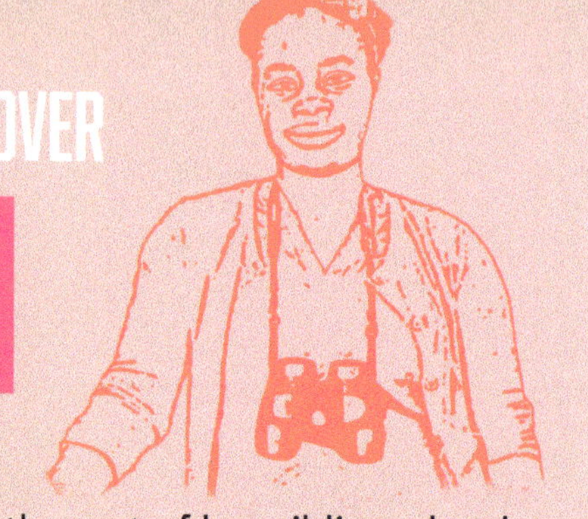

In the spring of 2020, Nicole Jackson was part of a core group of black scientists who launched the #BlackBirdersWeek movement. The initiative, which sought to amplify and encourage diverse participation in outdoor environments sans discrimination, won support from *Smithsonian* magazine, Forbes, CNN, NPR, the National Wildlife Federation, the National Audubon Society, and other organizations. Nicole also founded Black In National Parks Week in 2020, an initiative created to highlight, celebrate, and explore black experiences, history, and contributions in U.S. national parks.

Nicole Jackson was born in Cleveland, Ohio, on May 22, 1988. She is the third oldest of eleven children (eight girls and three boys). Sometime between the ages of five and six, Nicole and one sibling entered foster care, and both experienced abuse. To cope with the trauma derived from her caregivers, Nicole often ventured outside, which was the only place she felt safe.

> **"What I was going through with my foster parents, I didn't feel safe with them. I leaned on my sister a lot. She leaned on me. But I found comfort in being out in nature. That started in the backyard of the home that I stayed in."**

Nicole took in the trees that surrounded her and listened to the birds and squirrels that occupied them. It distracted her mind from what she endured in the foster home. In this way, nature was early therapy, and it would continue to play a central role in her life over the years. Nicole eventually reunited with her mother and the rest of her siblings, but her interest in the natural world only intensified.

She pursued the subject in school and learned a great deal about plants and various habitats, but her studies were broad. Anything nature-related drew her attention. In her spare time, Nicole consumed books and documentaries expounding on nature. For a moment, she believed that her career path would lead to being a teacher or librarian. Nicole also considered becoming a veterinarian and took pre-vet courses at The Ohio State University. But during her second year of college, she realized that veterinary medicine was not the answer.

A summer internship changed everything. While working with a few graduate students, Nicole conducted field research as part of a wildlife science program. She collected data on two types of birds: northern cardinals and Acadian flycatchers. With two months spent in the field, Nicole learned to identify various birds. She also learned the importance of bird habitats and what efforts were needed to help support them. The internship opened up a new world for her. Nicole wanted to extend her experience to others. That led to her exploring environmental education as a career path, which she has been doing for over a decade now. She is also going on four years as a Next Generation Advisory Council member with the National Parks Conservation Association (NPCA). The fellowship allowed her to advocate for and explore America's national parks.

Nicole is currently launching a coaching and consulting business focused on the mental health of black women, which will have nature, outdoor recreation, and self-care at its center. **U**

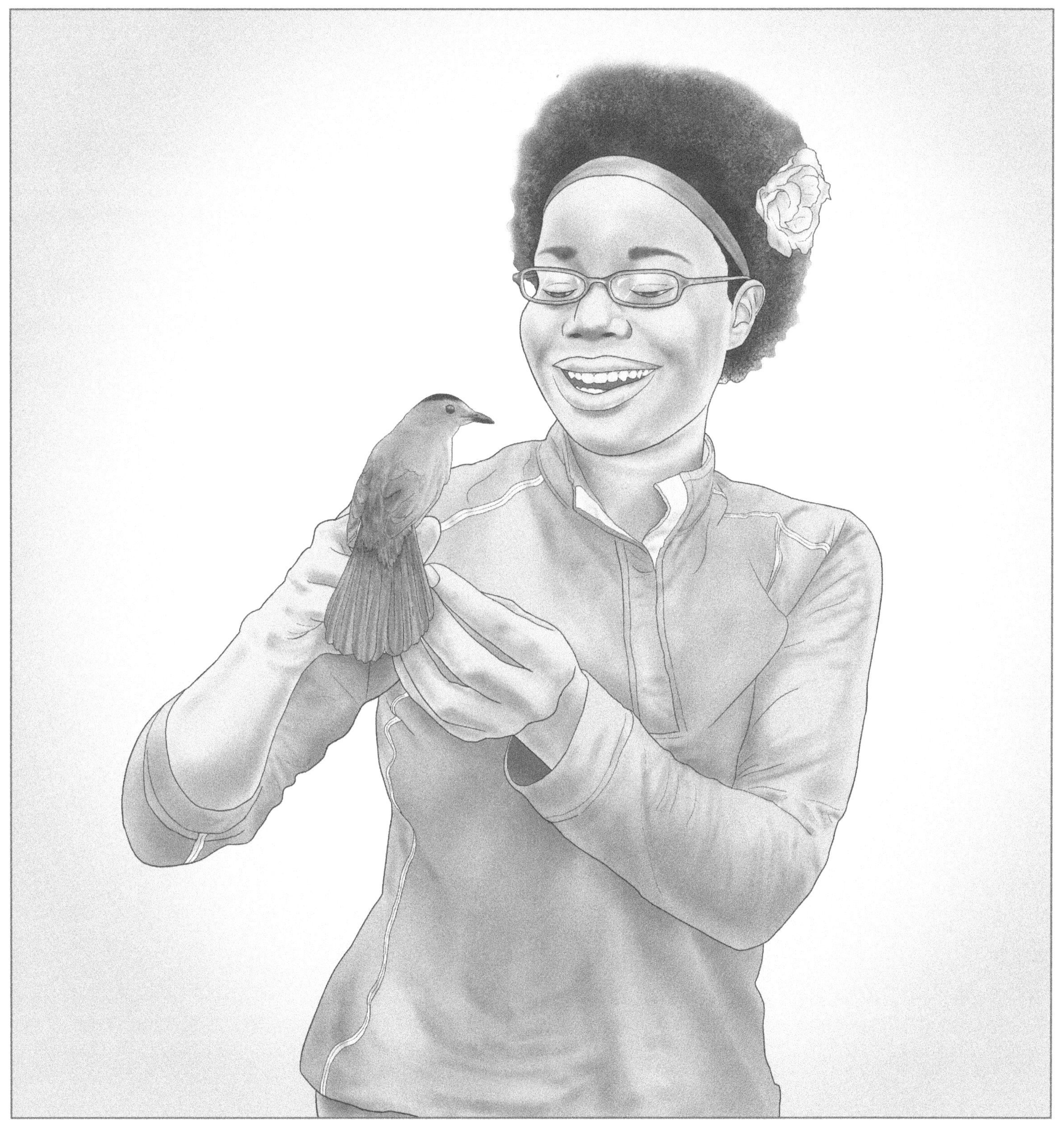

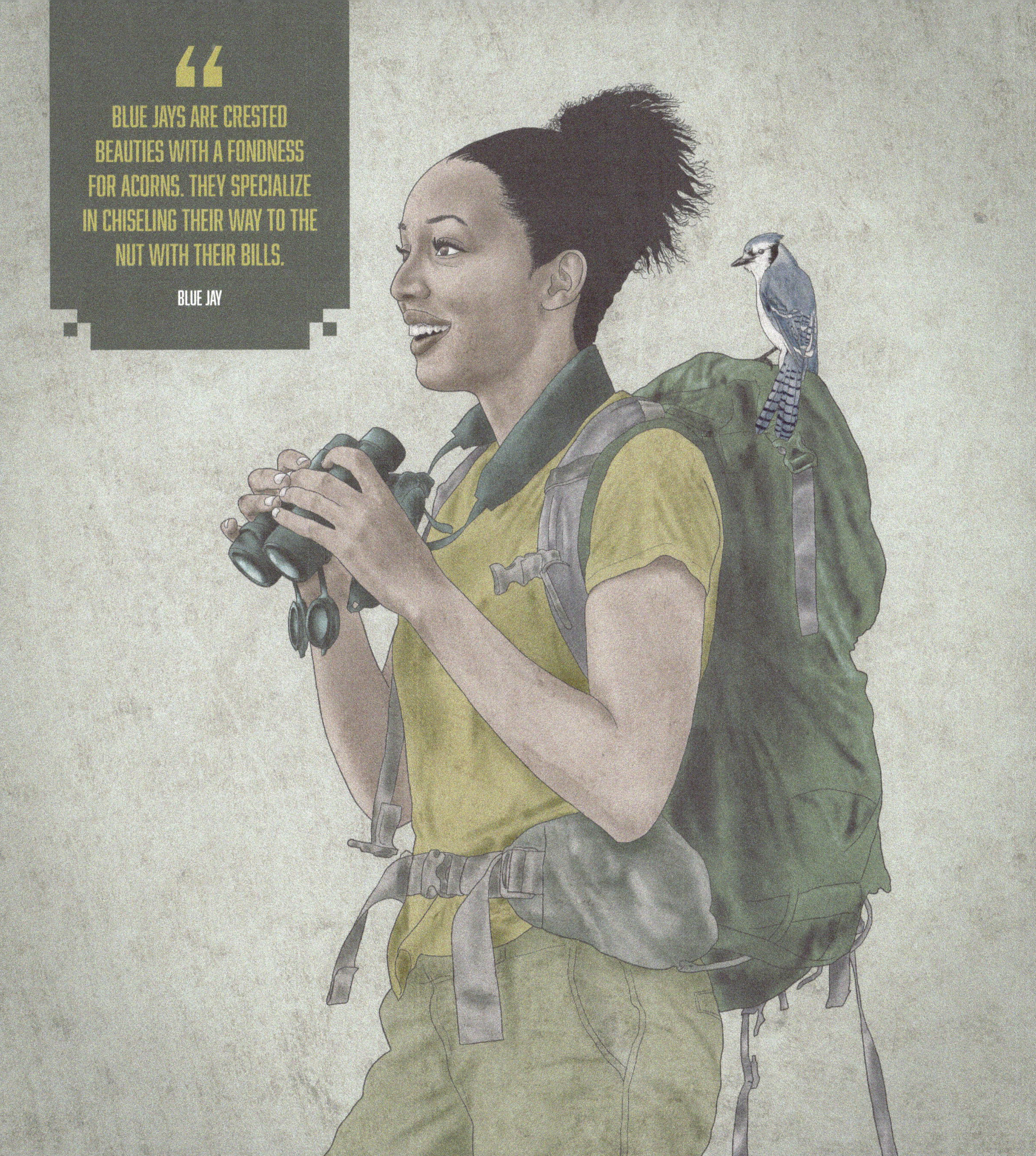

BLUE JAYS ARE CRESTED
BEAUTIES WITH A FONDNESS
FOR ACORNS. THEY SPECIALIZE
IN CHISELING THEIR WAY TO THE
NUT WITH THEIR BILLS.

BLUE JAY

CORINA NEWSOME

Corina Newsome served as the Community Engagement Manager at Georgia Audubon until 2022. She is now an Associate Conservation Scientist at the National Wildlife Federation. She has been a zoologist and a lab instructor at Georgia Southern University. She has also written articles for *Audubon* magazine and *BBC Wildlife*. Corina was also featured on NPR, PBS Nature, The Weather Channel, Black Entertainment Television, and in publications such as *Science* magazine, *The New Yorker*, *New York* magazine, and *The Washington Post*. Corina also co-organized the inaugural #BlackBirdersWeek and in 2018 she began conducting research and uncovered patterns that aided efforts to conserve the MacGillivray's seaside sparrow.

Corina Newsome was born in Philadelphia, Pennsylvania, on April 3, 1993. At the age of four, Corina wrote herself a note: "When I grow up, I want to be a scientist on bugs and animals." She consumed nature documentaries and followed the adventures of science communicators such as Steve Irwin. Corina's family nurtured her passion for wildlife by having her devour the National Geographic magazines and science books in their collection. Corina learned as much as possible about various species in the world. But because she had no connection to anyone working in wildlife, she concluded that becoming a veterinarian was the only path to fulfilling her passion.

A visit to the Philadelphia Zoo changed everything. A friend at church recognized Corina's interest in wildlife and told her to visit the zoo where his sister, Michelle Jamison, worked as a zookeeper. Corina called Michelle and arranged for a visit. Michelle immediately took Corina under her wing. Corina recalled:

"The moment that I saw her, I never even considered working with animals in conservation. I didn't even know what that looked like, let alone including someone who looked like me. The window was open and I could suddenly see the possibilities."

Corina admitted that Michelle caused her passion for wildlife to turn into a career. Corina received homeschooling up to fourth grade, then attended a charter school and middle school in Philadelphia. For ninth grade, her mother secured a scholarship that allowed Corina to attend Baldwin, an all-girl private school in a Philadelphia suburb called Bryn Mawr. The high school included academic rigor that not only prepared Corina for college but which she also applied to her later workflow. Corina left Pennsylvania to attend Malone University in northeast Ohio, where she majored in zoo and wildlife biology.

After receiving her bachelor's, Corina entered the workforce as a zookeeper, where she worked with over one hundred species of animals, many of which were birds. After three and a half years, she went back to school to obtain her master's. She graduated from Georgia Southern University in 2021 with a Master of Science in Biology degree. Her focus was ornithology or the study of birds. Today, Corina presents people with opportunities to contribute to bird conservation through direct participation. Her focus has been on communities filled with people who have been excluded from conservation efforts, mainly blacks and people of color. U

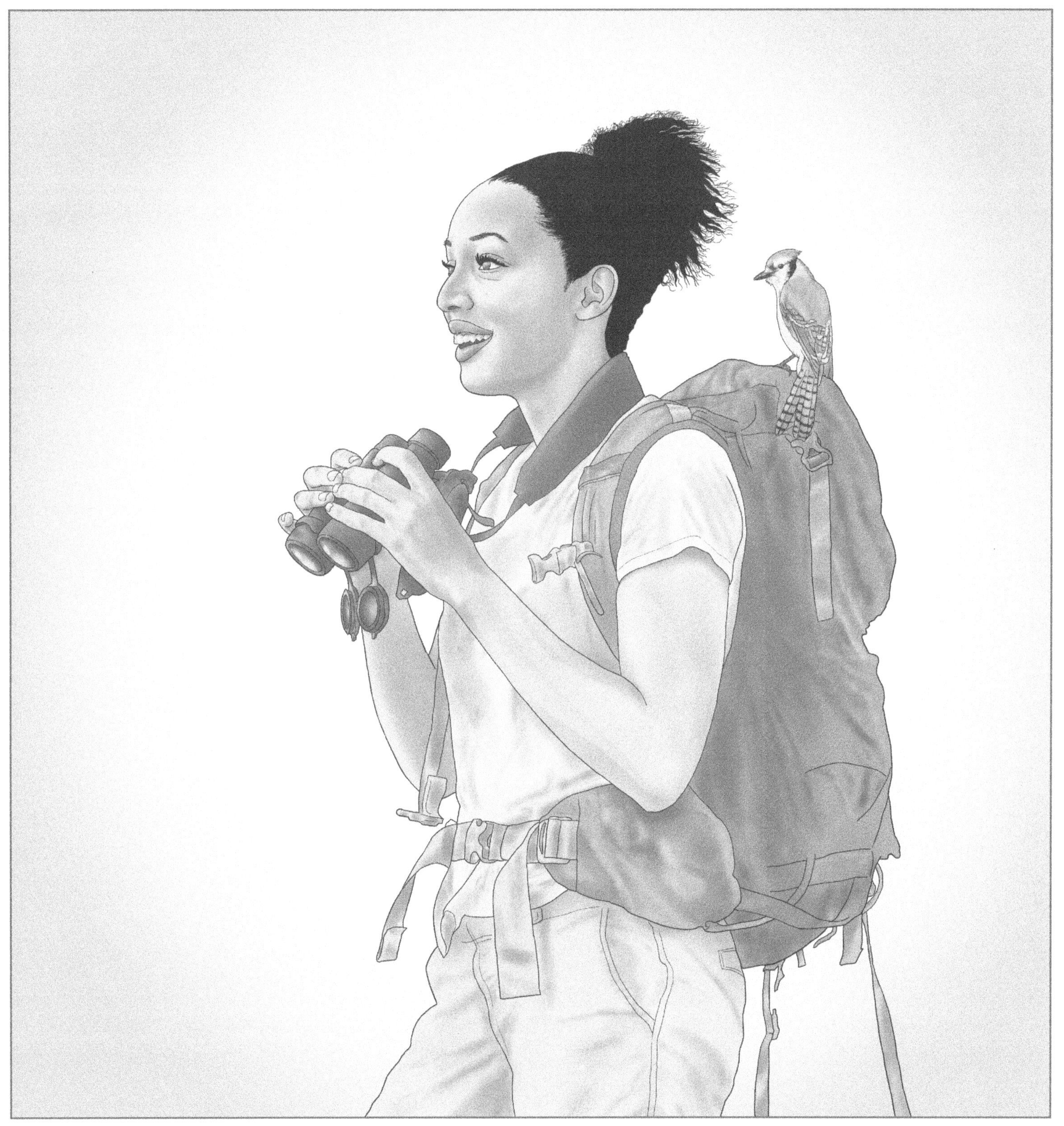

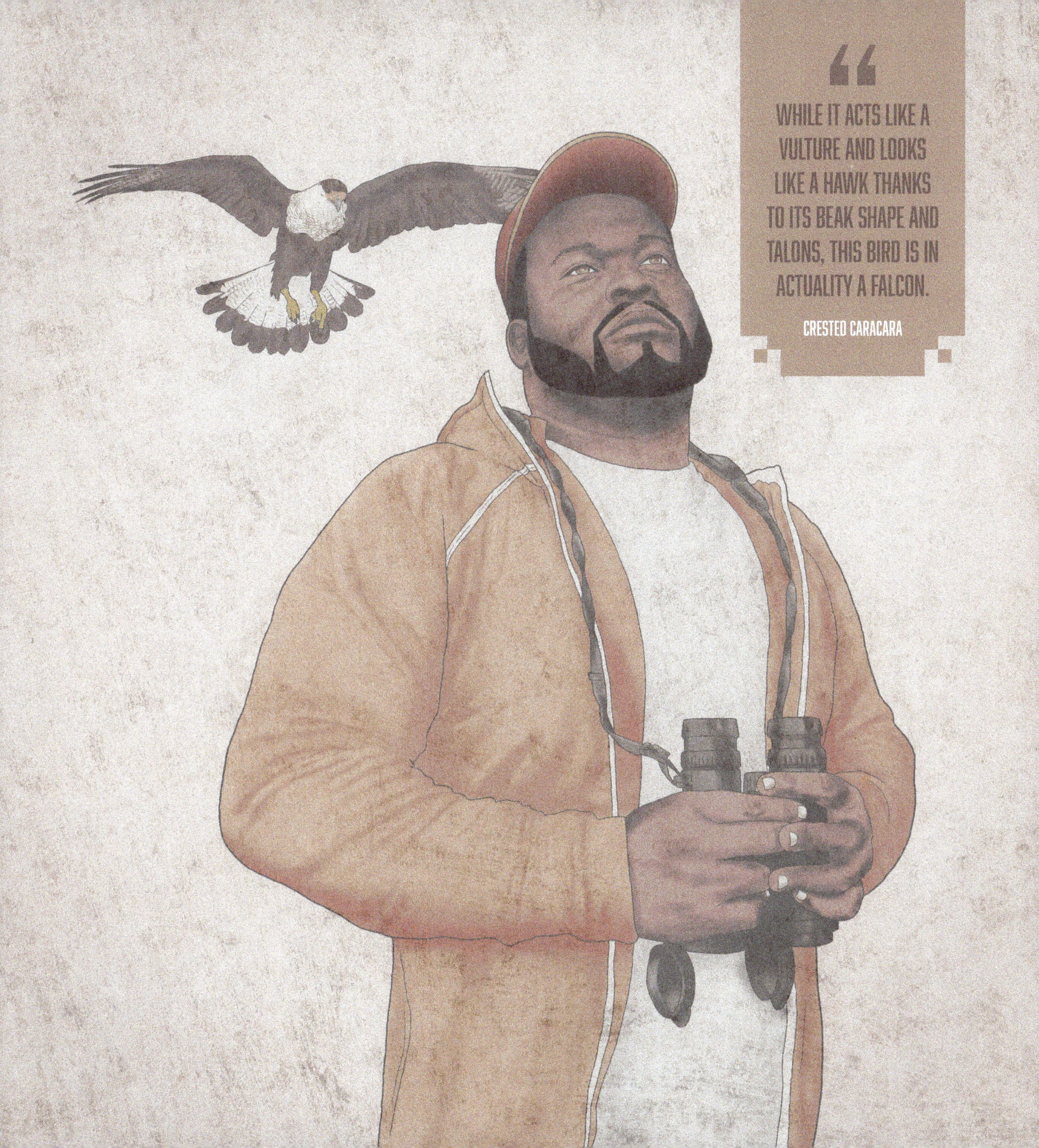

"
WHILE IT ACTS LIKE A VULTURE AND LOOKS LIKE A HAWK THANKS TO ITS BEAK SHAPE AND TALONS, THIS BIRD IS IN ACTUALITY A FALCON.
CRESTED CARACARA

ALEX TROUTMAN

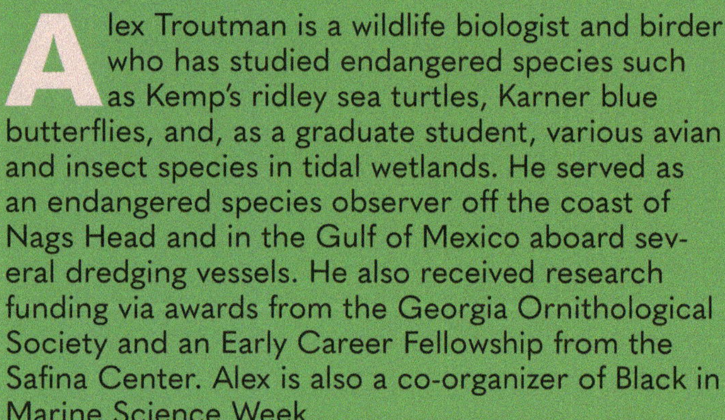

Alex Troutman is a wildlife biologist and birder who has studied endangered species such as Kemp's ridley sea turtles, Karner blue butterflies, and, as a graduate student, various avian and insect species in tidal wetlands. He served as an endangered species observer off the coast of Nags Head and in the Gulf of Mexico aboard several dredging vessels. He also received research funding via awards from the Georgia Ornithological Society and an Early Career Fellowship from the Safina Center. Alex is also a co-organizer of Black in Marine Science Week.

Alex Troutman was born the third of six children in Atlanta, Georgia, on September 25, 1990. His family moved to Austell, Georgia, in May 1994. His interest in nature and marine science began when he would spot great blue herons fishing nearby or across the lake during weekend fishing trips with his dad, brothers, and uncle. Red-tailed hawks soaring overhead with their tails aglow in the bright sun also drew his attention on those trips. His interest in nature was a constant distraction growing up. He admitted to taking over an hour to cut the quarter-acre yard because he was so fascinated with the animals scurrying out of the path of his lawnmower.

When he graduated from South Cobb High School, Alex attended Georgia Southern University and earned a bachelor's degree in biology in 2014. The following year, Alex began learning science communication after spending seven months working as a park ranger for Allegheny County, Pennsylvania, through the Student Conservation Association.

His first professional exposure to the marine field came when Alex worked as an environmental edu-cator for Zoo Atlanta and the Georgia Aquarium. For over six months, Alex taught lessons on marine life to school groups who visited the aquarium. He made a career transition in 2016, joining the U.S. Fish and Wildlife Service (USFWS) as a biological technician. He carried that experience to a similar position with the National Park Service, where he worked with nesting and stranded sea turtles at Padre Island National Seashore.

Alex has experienced racism on the job. When he worked for the Fish and Wildlife Service, a white guest who had no professional authority over him questioned him for being in the field. Despite his uniform, Alex de-escalated the situation by display-ing his official ID. While his career as a black wildlife biologist has had its ups and downs, with Alex being the only black employee at many organizations, Alex sees that oversight as an opportunity to pave the way for future black scientists. Others have also recognized the importance of his role in wildlife. Alex recalled:

> **"I was out working on the beach when a black family came up, introduced their children, and asked me to give an impromptu career speech about my job."**

Though shy and introverted as a child, Alex's science career helped him overcome his insecuri-ties. He went from being uncomfortable as a stand-out in a crowd to lecturing before an audience of hundreds. Alex plans to create a nonprofit that will open the natural resource field to people of color and citizens of low socioeconomic status. 🅄

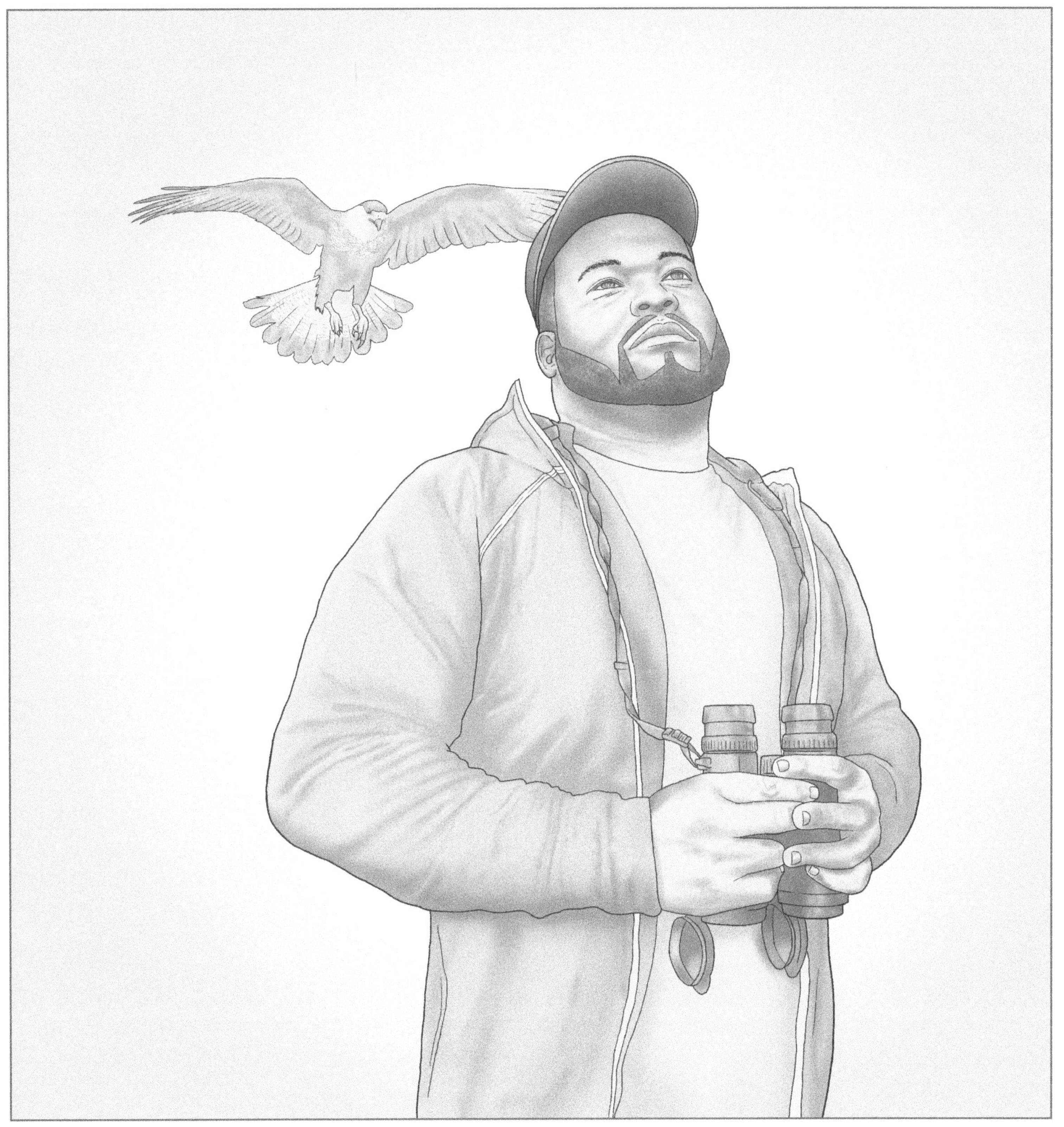

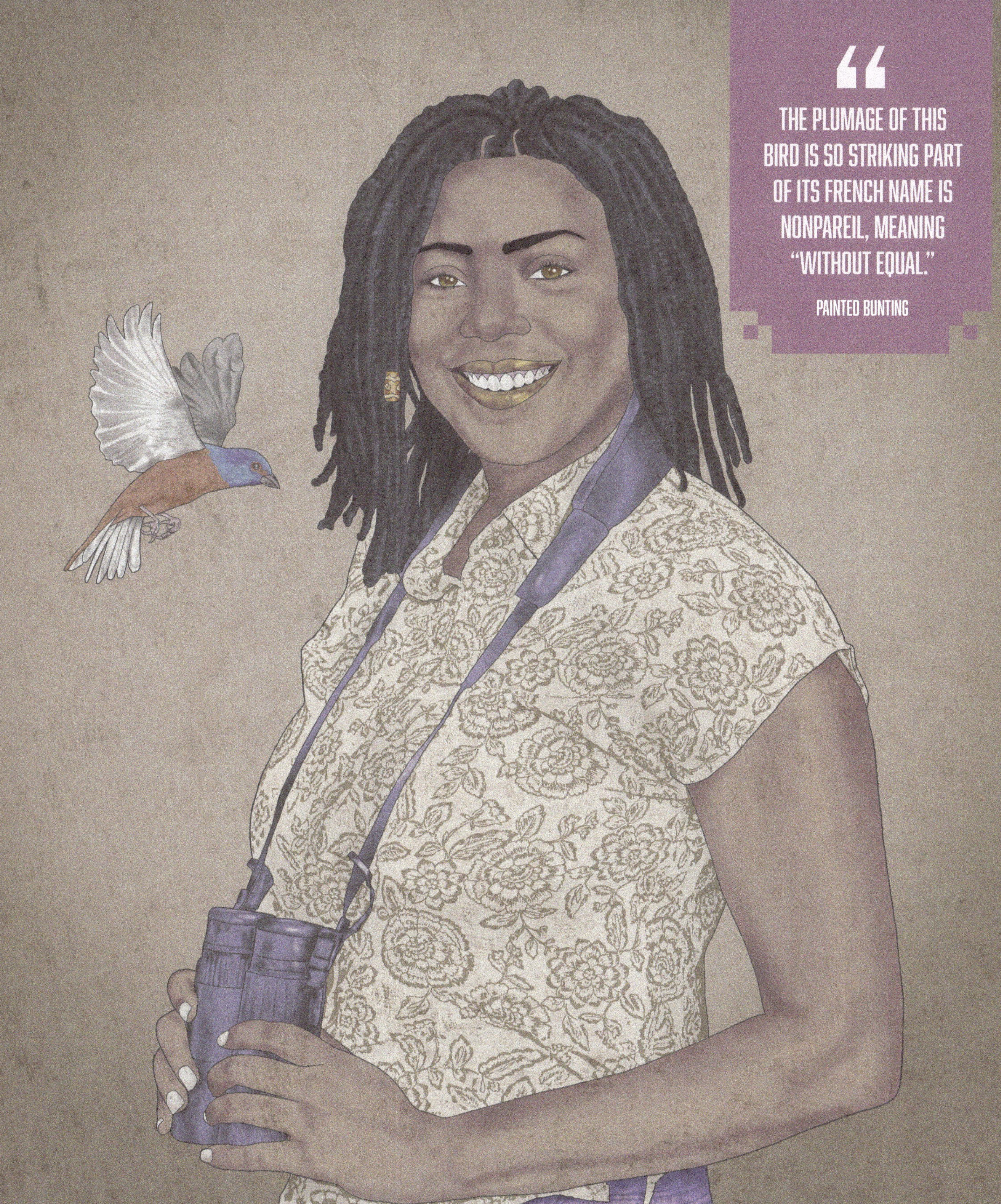

THE PLUMAGE OF THIS BIRD IS SO STRIKING PART OF ITS FRENCH NAME IS NONPAREIL, MEANING "WITHOUT EQUAL."

PAINTED BUNTING

DANIELLE BELLENY

Danielle Belleny is a wildlife biologist known for co-organizing the first #BlackBirdersWeek, which ran from May 31 to June 5, 2020. The event came in the wake of the murder of George Floyd and Christian Cooper's encounter with a racist woman in Central Park, both of which occurred on May 25, 2020. Danielle was part of a group chat that included a small number of black scientists who discussed the recent acts of racism and decided to do something about it. Danielle suggested they launch an Instagram account, and she offered to manage it.

"I ran the group's Instagram a little less than a year, maybe 9–10 months. I was just trying to organize and keep our heads on straight. I had some connections from my past, like Audubon Society, eBird, and Cornell Lab, and they reached out to us and became part of #BlackBirdersWeek."

Danielle Elizabeth Belleny was born in Dayton, Ohio, on August 8, 1994. As a child, she was passionate about nature. She enjoyed picking out snails from garden plants, chasing lizards, and creating personal ant colonies. On occasion, Danielle also helped her mother remove spiders from the house, and she did so gently. When she was three years old, her father retired from the Air Force, and the family moved to San Antonio, Texas. Her grandparents lived not far away in Austin on 14 acres that included dense woods. Danielle recalled spending several weeks in Austin during the summer exploring her grandparents' property in her quest to make discoveries in nature.

Up until the third grade, Danielle attended Village Parkway, a private school in San Antonio. She was homeschooled through fifth grade and returned to public school for her middle grades. When she attended Sandra Day O'Connor High School, she pursued a career in veterinary medicine through volunteer work. After visiting the Texas A&M College of Veterinary Medicine & Biomedical Sciences, she changed her mind. Her siblings had obtained degrees from the University of Houston, so she decided to follow suit. But she tired of the biology courses and the general path she had taken. Her dad helped her restructure, and they mapped out a new direction centered on wildlife management at Texas A&M University–Kingsville.

It was at A&M in South Texas that Danielle got "hooked" into birding, as she put it. The diversity of birds grabbed her attention, and she realized she was on the right path. As her passion for birds and wildlife blossomed, Danielle aided graduate students in their studies. She became a graduate student also but left A&M to attend Tarleton State University in Stephenville, Texas. Like A&M in the south, Tarleton State was situated in a middle-of-nowhere town, this time in the north. Danielle studied northern bobwhite—or Virginia quail—while pursuing her master's degree. After graduation, Danielle passed up opportunities she deemed compromises, such as consulting on pipeline projects. She eventually spent a year with the Martha's Vineyard Land Bank Commission and is now working as a wildlife biologist for Plateau Land & Wildlife Management in Austin, Texas. **U**

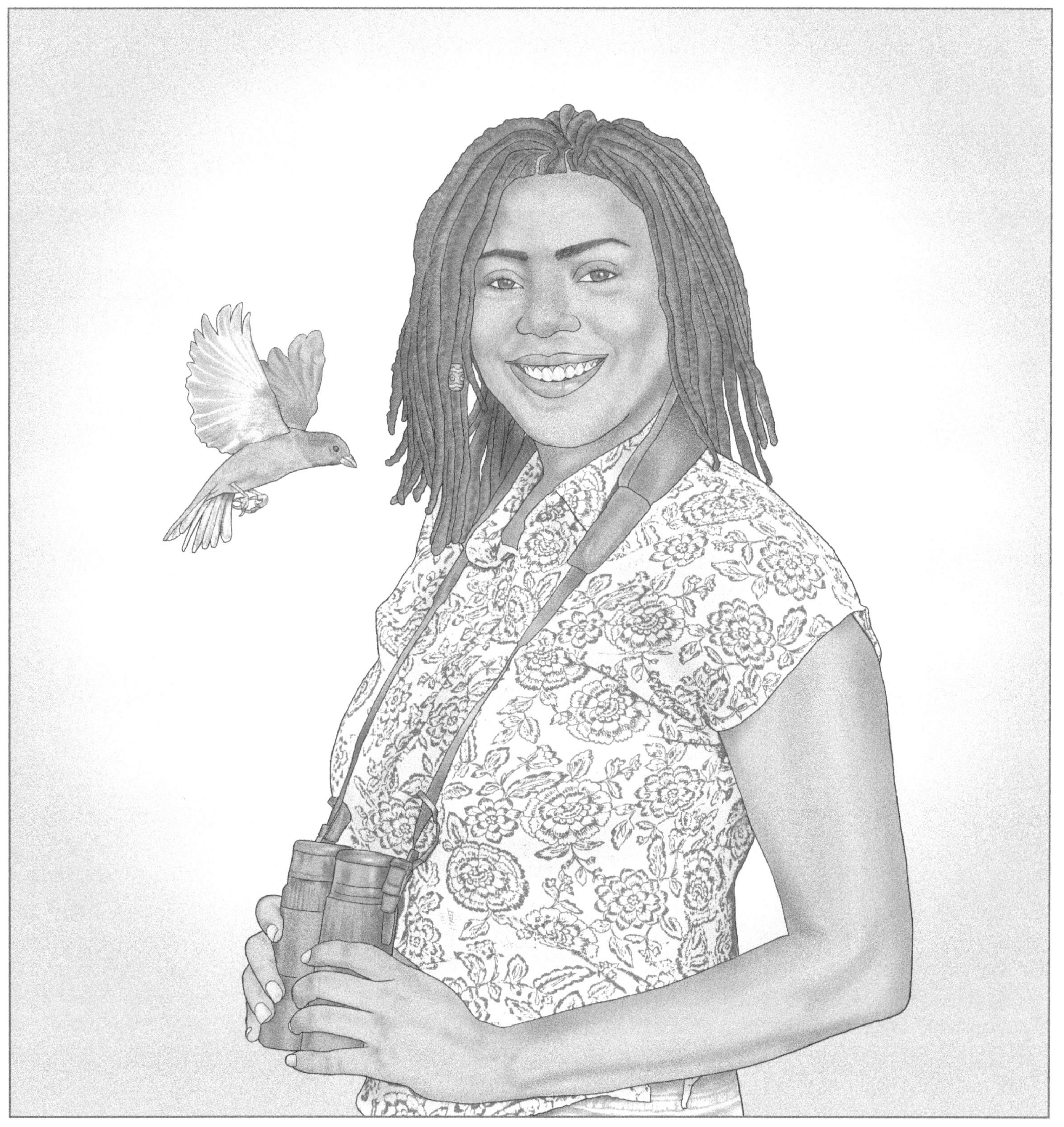

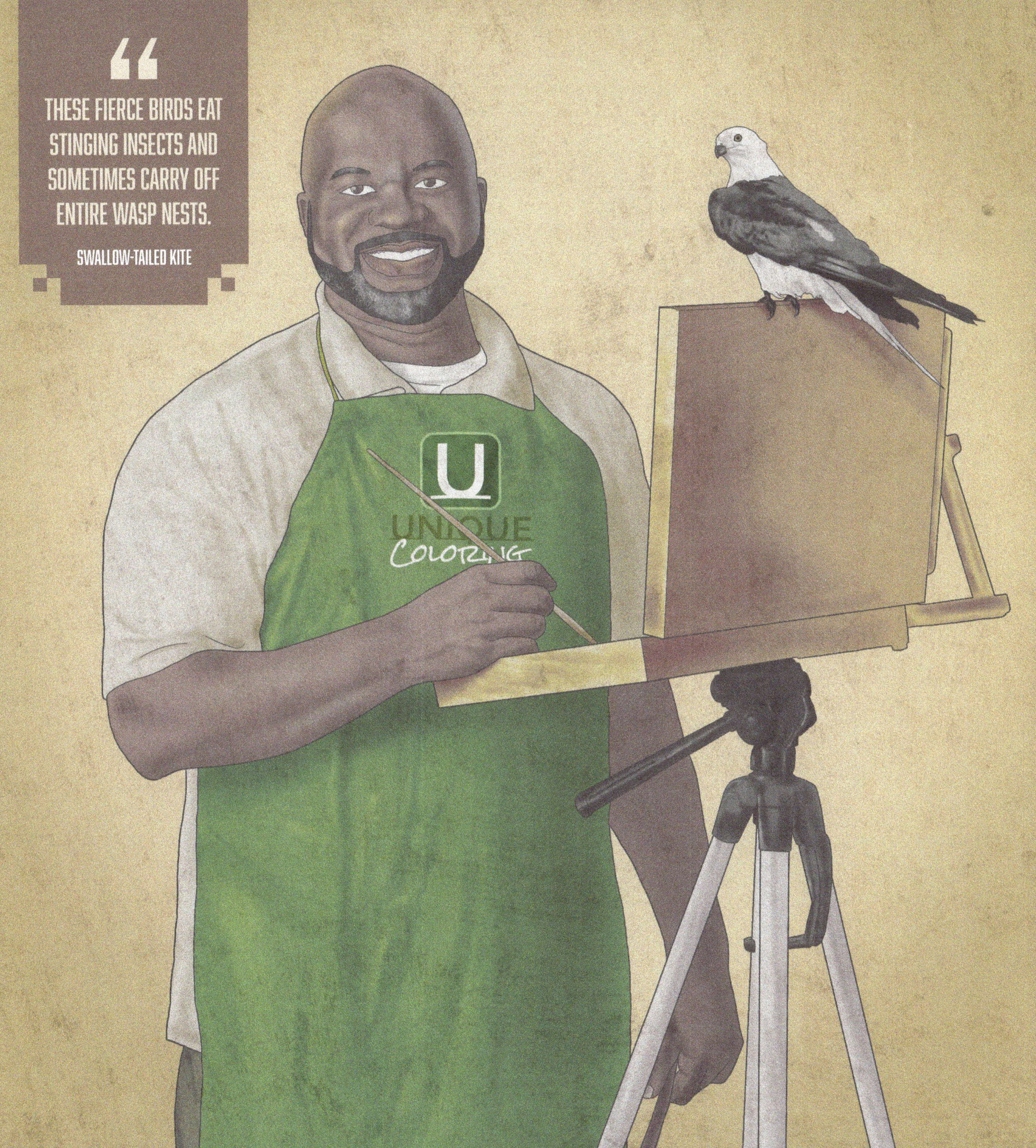
"
THESE FIERCE BIRDS EAT STINGING INSECTS AND SOMETIMES CARRY OFF ENTIRE WASP NESTS.
SWALLOW-TAILED KITE
UNIQUE
COLORING

TIMOTHY JOE

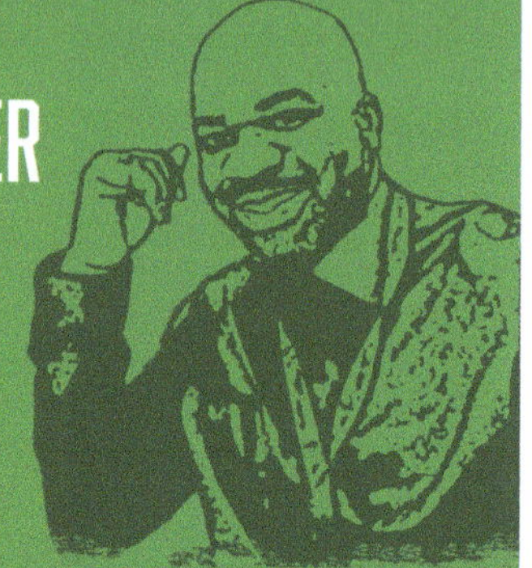

Timothy Joe is a self-taught representational artist and painting instructor from Alabama's Black Belt region. His rural roots are reflected in his art, as is his desire to preserve the landscape he grew up with. He specializes in painting onsite in the great outdoors, en plein air, and, beginning with the Hale County Black Belt Birding Tour in 2019—which happened on his family farm—has held live art demonstrations that have extended his passion for nature to others.

Timothy Michael Joe was born in Greensboro, Alabama, on August 21, 1982. His parents are Cornelius and Leola Joe. Timothy grew up on a 200-acre farm in Newbern, Alabama, purchased by his family in the early 1900s. The farm is in Alabama's Black Belt region, which originally referred to the rich, black topsoil found there and the enslaved black Americans who worked the fields when cotton agriculture dominated. With the spread of cotton-producing farms, the Black Belt region extended its reach, eventually encompassing lands in Georgia, Mississippi, and Louisiana.

Timothy became interested in art at age four. His mother brought home groceries in brown paper bags, which she left on the floor for Timothy to color using crayons. Timothy desired to paint after seeing Bob Ross on television. In an interview with artist and environmental educator Bethan Burton, Timothy spoke about the impact Bob Ross had on him:

"It was just him saying, 'you can do this too,' and I believed him. He really took art, which was something on a high shelf that a lot of people couldn't reach, and put it down to a level for anybody who desired to paint or draw."

Timothy's love of nature also developed on the family farm, with its pristine pastures, deeply wooded areas, and streams and ponds teeming with abundant birdlife. He was also attracted to neighbors' gardens and local settings with old, rustic structures, the latter of which figures prominently in his current portfolio.

Timothy began painting various birds as part of his nature journaling using watercolor, gouache, oils, and pastels. While Timothy was harvesting on the family farm, Mississippi kites and swallow-tailed kites swooped down to catch dragonflies in midair during the hay season. That struck him. It wasn't long before avid birders noted the timing and stopped by to catch sight of the kites from a distance. The Joe family realized an opportunity and opened the farm to bird tours run by Timothy's younger brother Christopher. Timothy has since hosted a few himself, in addition to leading nature journaling workshops for Alabama Audubon.

For his piece *Warm Welcome*, Timothy was a Pastel Spotlight artist in the August/September 2021 issue of *PleinAir* magazine. He won an award in the first annual Mountain View Americana Art Competition held in South Carolina and gave a gouache painting demo during the 2021 International Nature Journal Week. Timothy and his brother Christopher appeared in *Barriers to Bridges*, a documentary presented by the Alabama Rivers Alliance film fellowship program Southern Exposure. The film, directed by Robin Bean Crane, was a 2021 EarthxFilm award winner. Ⓤ

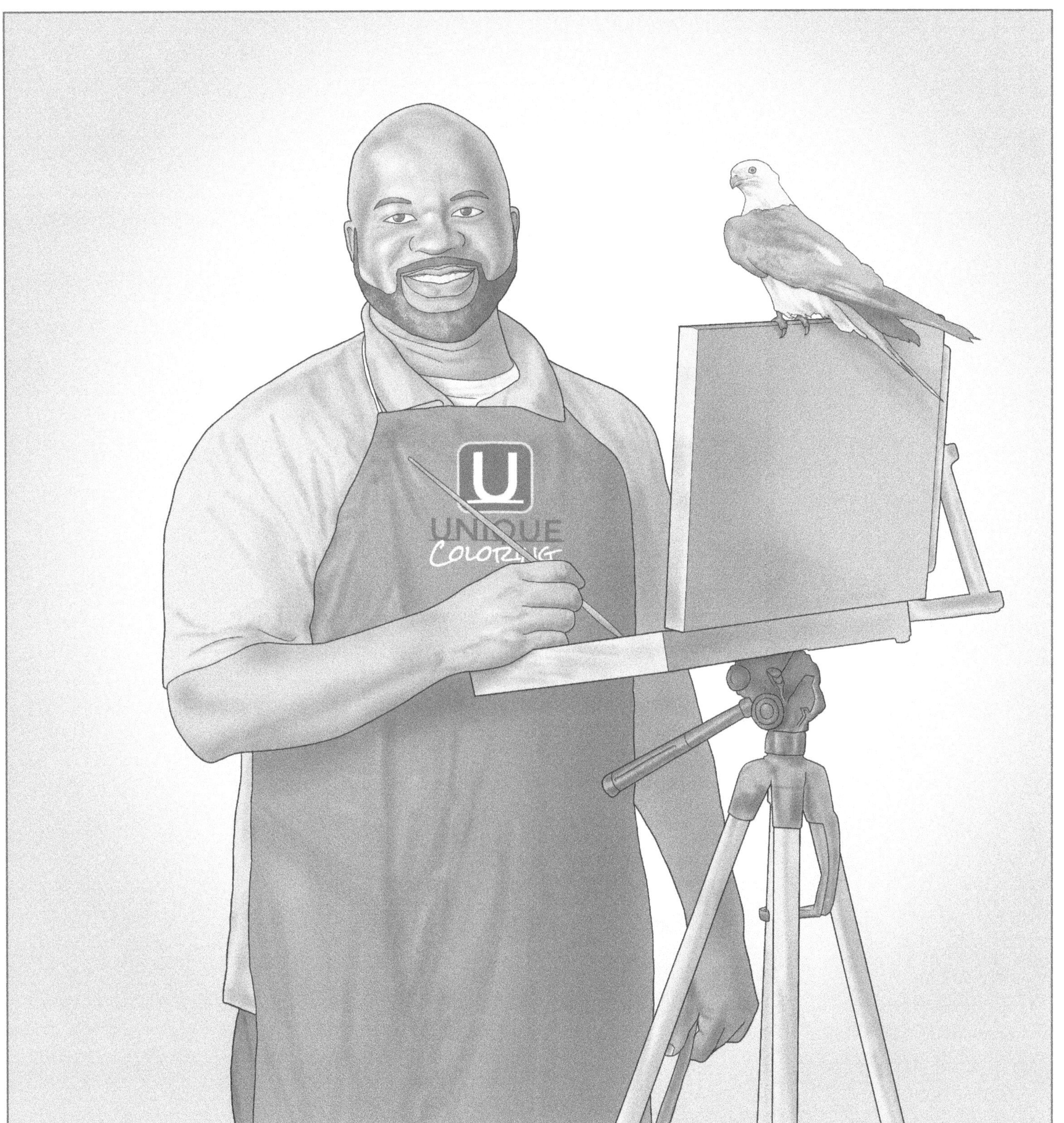

U
UNIQUE
COLORING

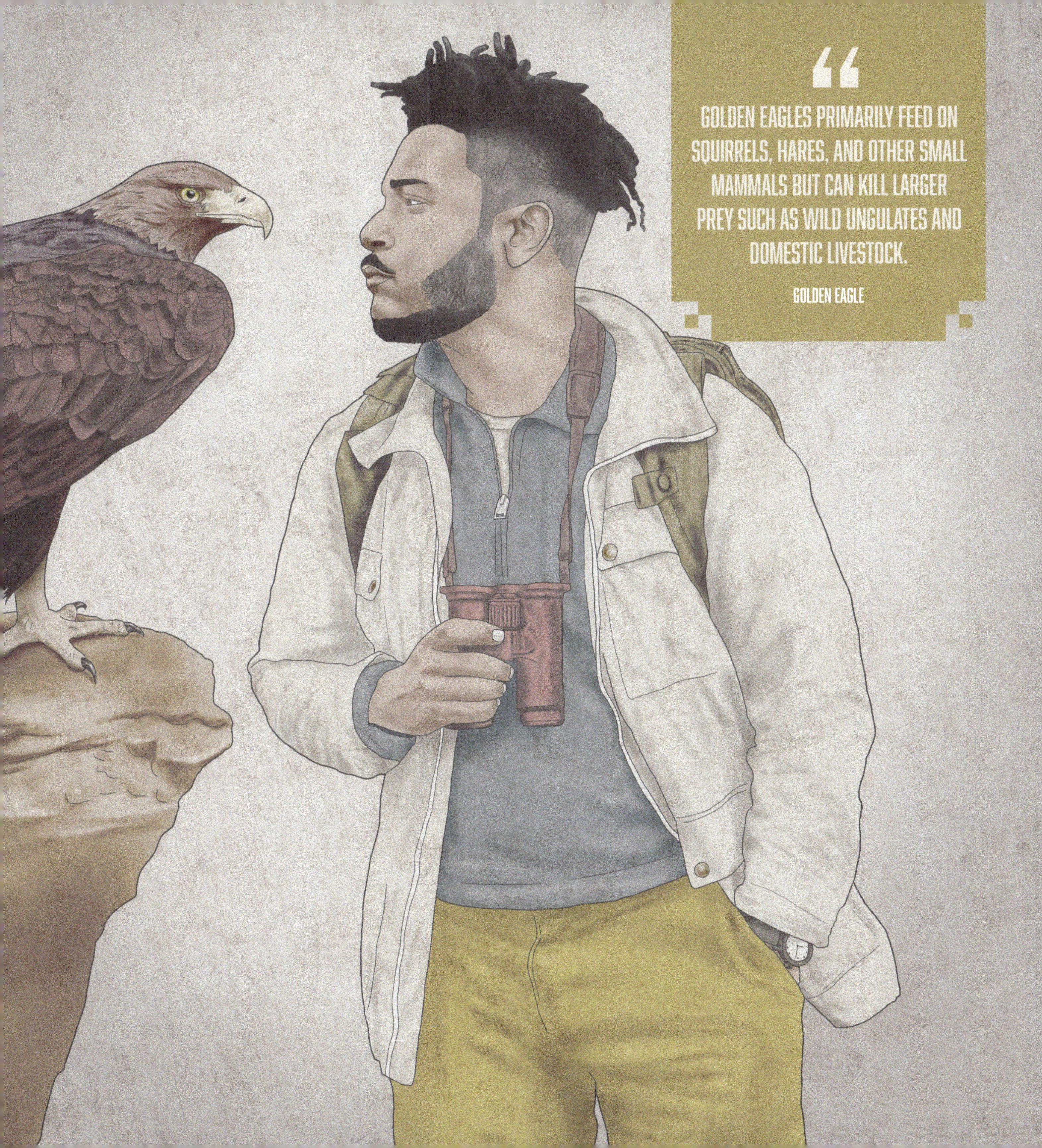
GOLDEN EAGLES PRIMARILY FEED ON SQUIRRELS, HARES, AND OTHER SMALL MAMMALS BUT CAN KILL LARGER PREY SUCH AS WILD UNGULATES AND DOMESTIC LIVESTOCK.
GOLDEN EAGLE

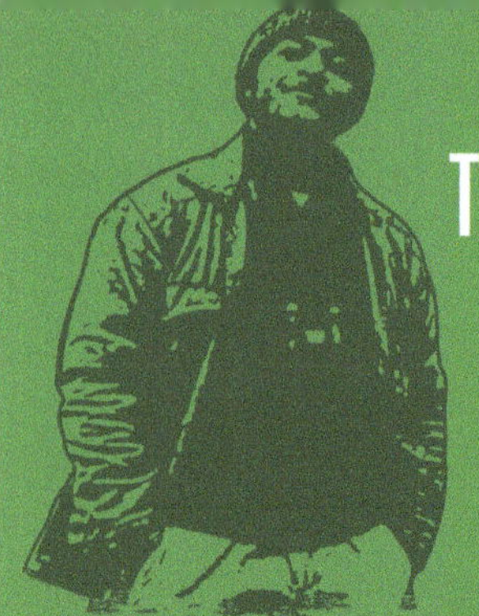

TOLGA AKTAS

Tolga Aktas—a conservation biologist based in the United Kingdom—is part Jamaican part Turkish Cypriot. His upbringing led to a love of nature that he pursued as a career later in life. Tolga has since traveled to Africa, Borneo, and distant regions of the United Kingdom to conduct field research and volunteer for various wildlife conversation projects.

Tolga Aktas was born in London, United Kingdom, on January 19, 1992, the fourth of five children. His mother is from Clarendon, a parish in Jamaica, and his father is from Cihangir, a village in Northern Cyprus. Tolga grew up in South London in the United Kingdom, where he spent much of his childhood, but he traveled to Jamaica and North Cyprus often. Tolga was introduced to various ecosystems and habitats while visiting the two countries. Though he was drawn to nature as a child and grew up surrounded by animals, he did not realize that one could have a career in wildlife. Nature documentaries presented by Steve Irwin and Sir David Attenborough gave him a new outlook.

Tolga did not pursue wildlife studies in his youth due to a lack of resources, and because he saw no wildlife presenters or conservationists who bore his skin color, he considered the career a lost cause. His outlook grew bleak, and his grades suffered as a result. Tolga left secondary school and found work in an apprenticeship as an electrical engineer, but he had no passion for that field.

For close to a year, Tolga often skipped lunch with the other engineers to visit a pet store, where he felt at home as he stroked various animals. He recalled his love of nature and began to reconsider his career choice. During an interview on *The Outdoors Fix* podcast, Tolga said:

"Then after some more time thinking about it I just stormed up to the top floor of our engineering office and just said to the manager, 'I'm gonna leave.'"

And he did leave. Tolga started doing extensive research and launched into volunteer work, which started at Surrey Docks Farm on the Thames in London, 15 minutes walking distance from his house. He was finally getting work experience in his field of choice. Tolga volunteered for nearly two years, and then he transitioned to Battersea Park Children's Zoo, where his education in conservation began. Tolga also worked at a monkey sanctuary in Cornwall, UK, a wolf sanctuary in Reading, UK, and a turtle conservation and research project in Northern Cyprus near his family's village home.

Tolga earned an advanced diploma in animal management from Capel Manor College and followed that up with a bachelor's in animal biology from the University of Gloucestershire. While pursuing his degree, Tolga traveled to KwaZulu-Natal in Africa to work with endangered species in collaboration with Wildlife ACT, a non-profit trust. His field research on wild dogs and lions was foundational to his thesis. Tolga loves spending time in natural settings looking for birds and other wildlife. He frequents places like Epping Forest—the ancient woodland that straddles the border between London and Essex—and Highnam Woods near his current home in Gloucestershire. U

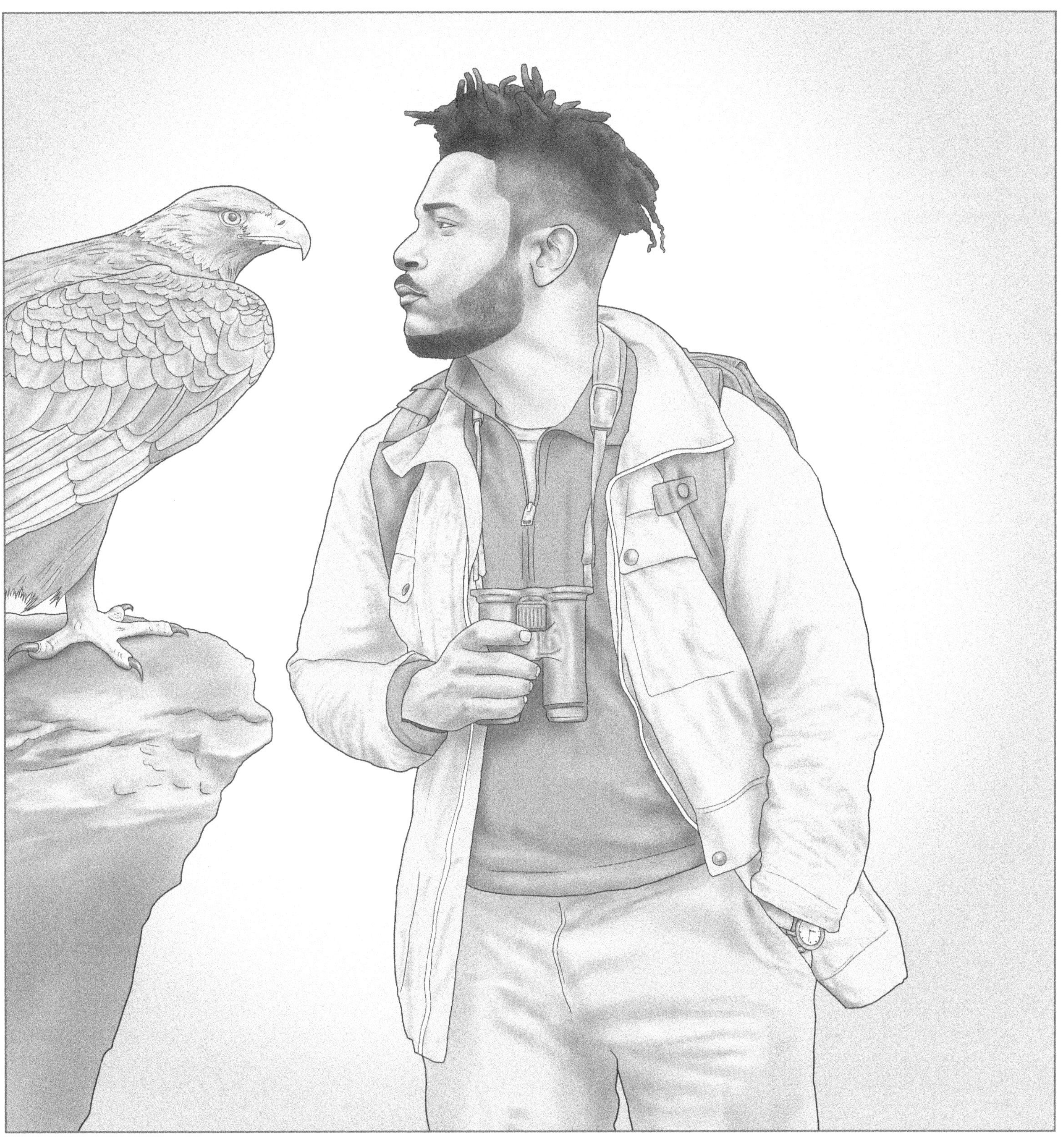

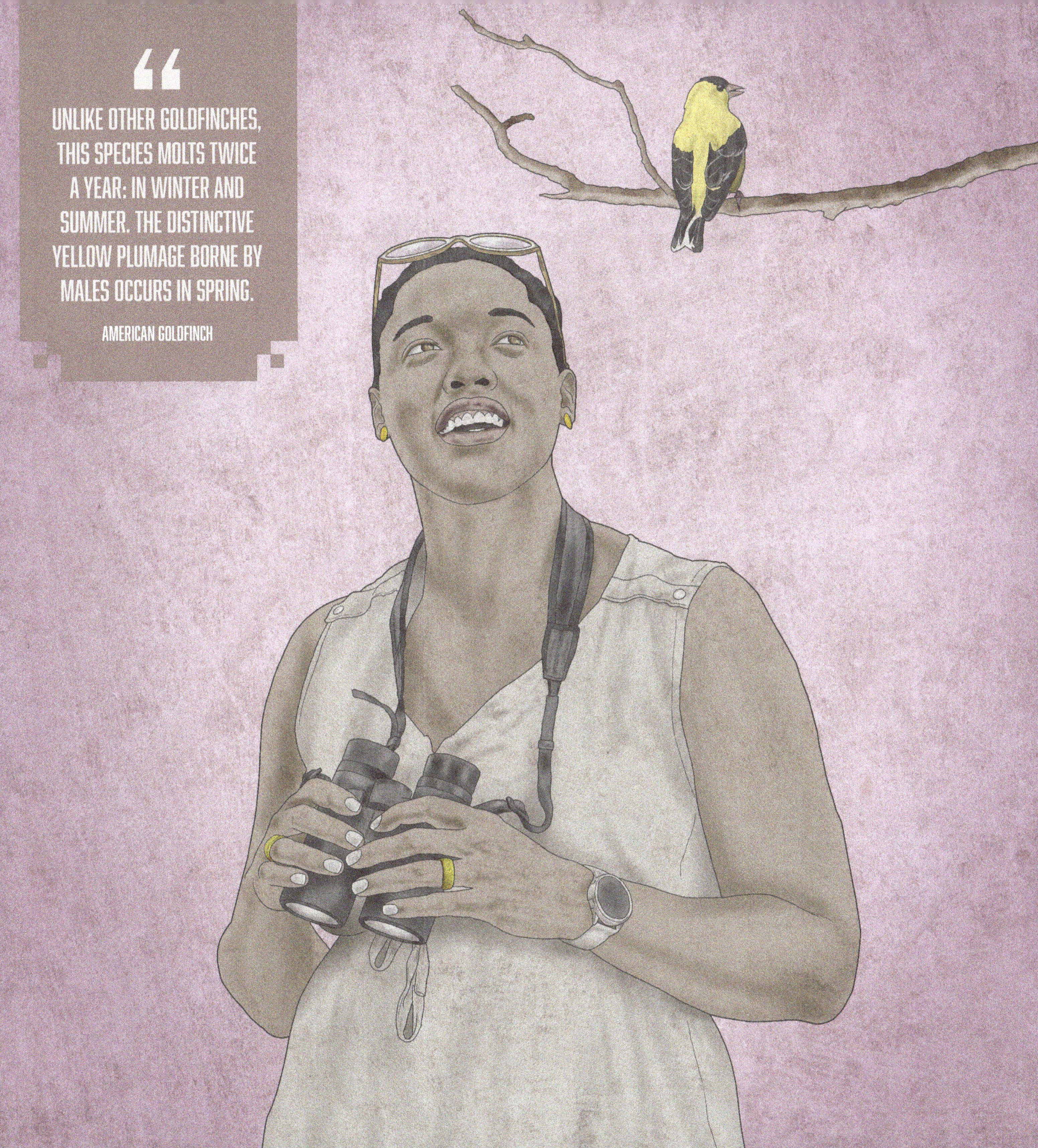
UNLIKE OTHER GOLDFINCHES, THIS SPECIES MOLTS TWICE A YEAR: IN WINTER AND SUMMER. THE DISTINCTIVE YELLOW PLUMAGE BORNE BY MALES OCCURS IN SPRING.
AMERICAN GOLDFINCH

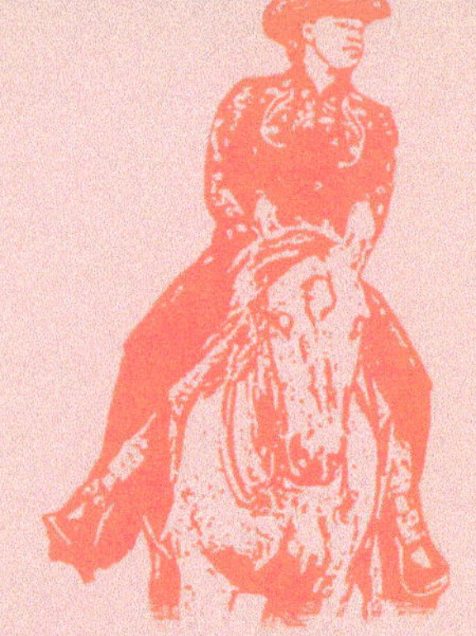

BRIANNA AMINGWA

Brianna Amingwa is working to create change both locally and nationally in her role as leader of the U.S. Fish and Wildlife Service's Environmental Education Community of Practice. The teachers and students she works with actively participate and engage in shared learning that fosters environmental literacy and sustainability practices.

Brianna Amingwa was born in Detroit, Michigan, on November 27, 1992, to Elvis and Angela Patrick. As a girl scout, Brianna got to ride horses on a farm and immediately fell in love. Later, an acquaintance of her grandmother's introduced them to a lawyer named Doug Lewis, who is director of legal services at the University of Michigan. Doug was a black cowboy with a large farm in Southeast Michigan that was open to urban youths who wanted to volunteer their time and services in exchange for horseback riding lessons. Doug took Brianna and several children from the city under his wings and taught them about horses. Riding in the woods was an awakening experience for Brianna, as it was her true introduction to nature.

She rode with Doug through high school, then applied to Michigan State University and majored in animal science, which centered on livestock studies. During her freshman year, Brianna attended a career fair provided by Minorities in Agriculture, Natural Resources and Related Sciences (MANRRS), a national organization that promotes academic and professional advancement by empowering ethnic minorities in those fields. A representative of the Student Conservation Association approached her for an interview. That led to an internship with the U.S. Fish and Wildlife Service, where she worked in wildlife refuges. During our interview, Brianna revealed:

"In my first summer internship, a biology internship, they had me working outside all day, every day. Daniel, I thought I was going to die. [We both laugh.] I was so scared because I was out in the marsh searching for these little prairie orchids and was totally overwhelmed and unprepared for working by myself out there. I'm wearing waders and sweating. It was intense."

One day, she worked with the visitors' services team and a park ranger, Laura Bonneau, required her assistance on a children's program called Nature Tots. Brianna interacted with children in rural Ohio and taught them about nature, an experience she thoroughly enjoyed. Laura also took Brianna out birding some mornings, and Brianna remembers the first bird Laura taught her about: the goldfinch. Laura told her to note the bouncing flight pattern and listen for the distinctive call they make, which sounds like "potato chip." Brianna became an avid birder after that.

A career conversion led to Brianna working at a wildlife refuge in Iowa, where she engaged in visitors' services and education and school programming. She is currently the education supervisor at John Heinz National Wildlife Refuge at Tinicum, the first urban wildlife refuge in the United States, located in Philadelphia. Brianna works directly with local teachers and minority students from the city, helping them to forge deep connections with their local environment. U

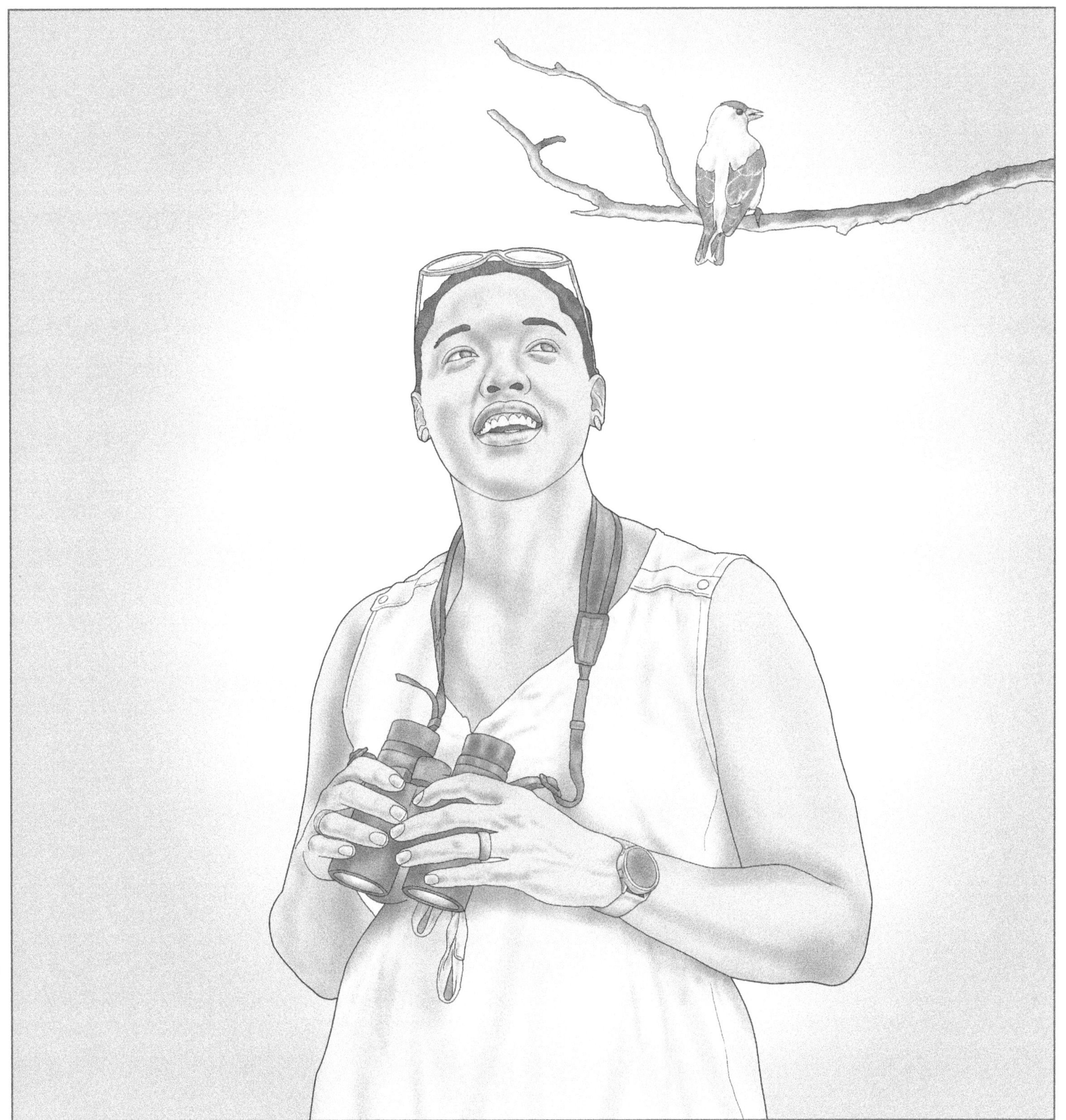

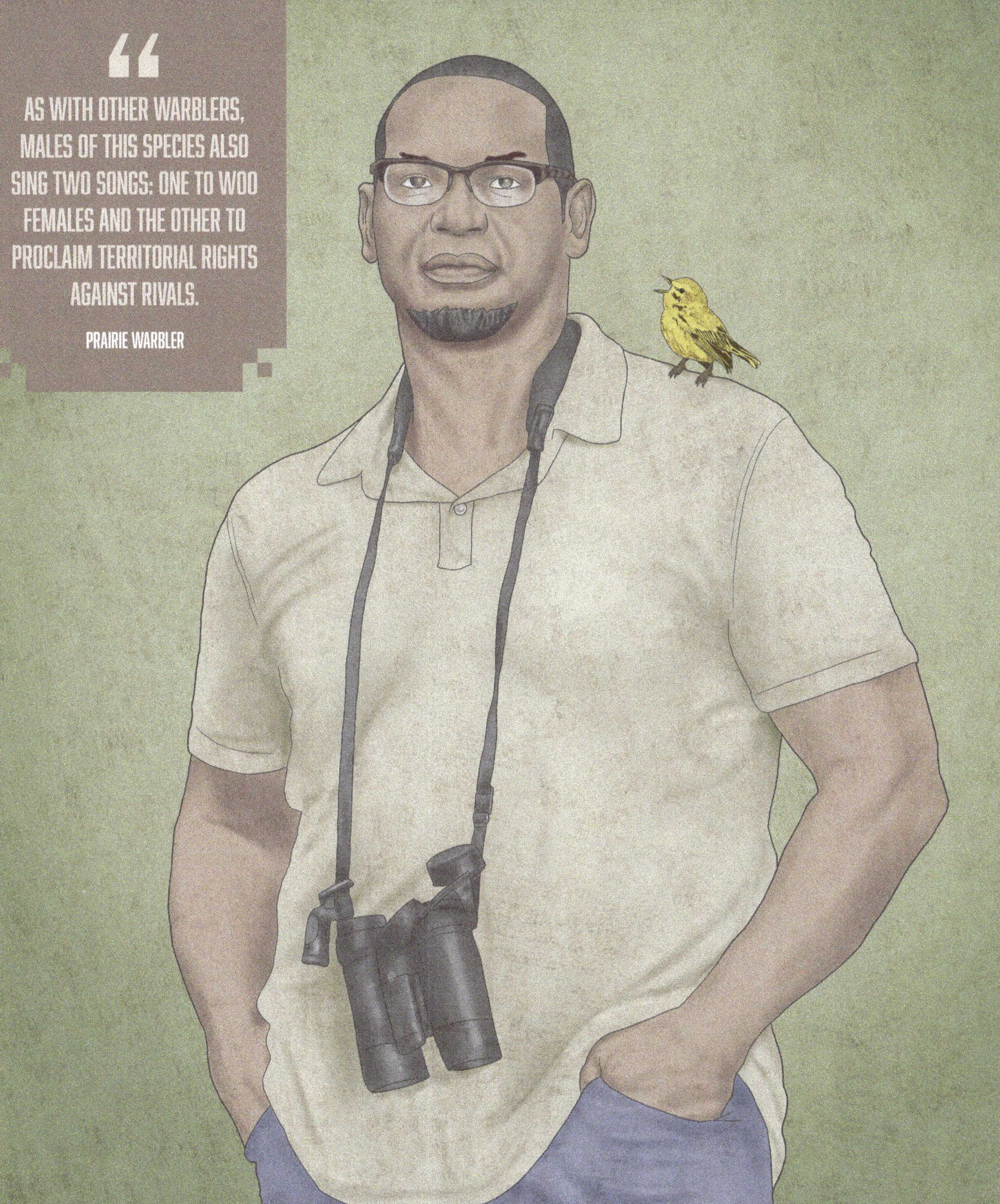
"
AS WITH OTHER WARBLERS, MALES OF THIS SPECIES ALSO SING TWO SONGS: ONE TO WOO FEMALES AND THE OTHER TO PROCLAIM TERRITORIAL RIGHTS AGAINST RIVALS.
PRAIRIE WARBLER

J. DREW LANHAM

Dr. J. Drew Lanham wrote an essay for a 2013 issue of *Orion* magazine titled, "9 Rules for the Black Birdwatcher." The article quickly led to a short video of the same name, which resonated with black birders throughout the country. Drew wrote essays and poetry for other publications, including *Wilderness*, *Flycatcher*, *Slate*, *Newsweek*, *Vanity Fair*, *Audubon*, and others. In 2018, he was named Poet Laureate of Edgefield, South Carolina, and in 2019, he released a poetry collection, *Sparrow Envy—Poems*. Drew is the author of the award-winning *The Home Place: Memoirs of a Colored Man's Love Affair with Nature*. Drew teaches wildlife ecology and holds an Alumni Distinguished Professorship at Clemson University. In 2012, he was named an Alumni Master Teacher.

Joseph Drew Lanham was born in South Carolina in January 1965. He is the second of four children. He has a brother named Jock and two sisters named Jennifer and Julia. On his paternal side, he descends from an enslaved man named Harry, whose owners brought him to Edgefield, South Carolina, in 1790. Drew's father was James Hoover Lanham, a jack of all trades who taught seventh- and eighth-grade earth science. His mother, Willie May, taught biology and math. Though he did not get to know his grandfather, Joseph Samuel Lanham (affectionately called Daddy Joe), Drew had great respect for him. After Daddy Joe died, Drew divided his time between his grandmother Mamatha's old house—known as the Ramshackle—and his parents' ranch, dubbed the Home Place.

Drew grew up surrounded by abundant wildlife, and he read everything he could on the subject. Drew borrowed books from the library, pored through encyclopedias, consulted an almanac, and studied brief field guide descriptions and images. He wrote in his 2016 memoir, *The Home Place*:

> **"I went back outdoors, where I walked, stalked, and waited to see as many wild things as I could. I collected tadpoles to watch them grow into froglets; I caught butterflies and gazed into their thousand-lensed eyes. Birds were everywhere and as I learned to identify them by sight their songs sunk into my psyche, too. Nature was often the first and last thing on my mind, morning to night."**

Drew fostered his love of birds and wildlife through academia. He earned three degrees from the same University, Clemson, in South Carolina. A bachelor's and master's in zoology came in 1988 and 1990, respectively, while he obtained his PhD in forest resources in 1997. As a natural progression, Drew joined the Clemson faculty and spent over twenty years structuring and teaching courses, conducting research, and performing outreach. Drew is involved in woodland ecology, forest biodiversity, conservation ornithology, and other passions. He sits on several conservation boards, including Audubon South Carolina, South Carolina Wildlife Federation, the Aldo Leopold Foundation, the American Birding Association, and BirdNote. Drew has mentored over 40 graduate students in his career. And he continues to advocate for diversity in birding and outdoor recreation. U

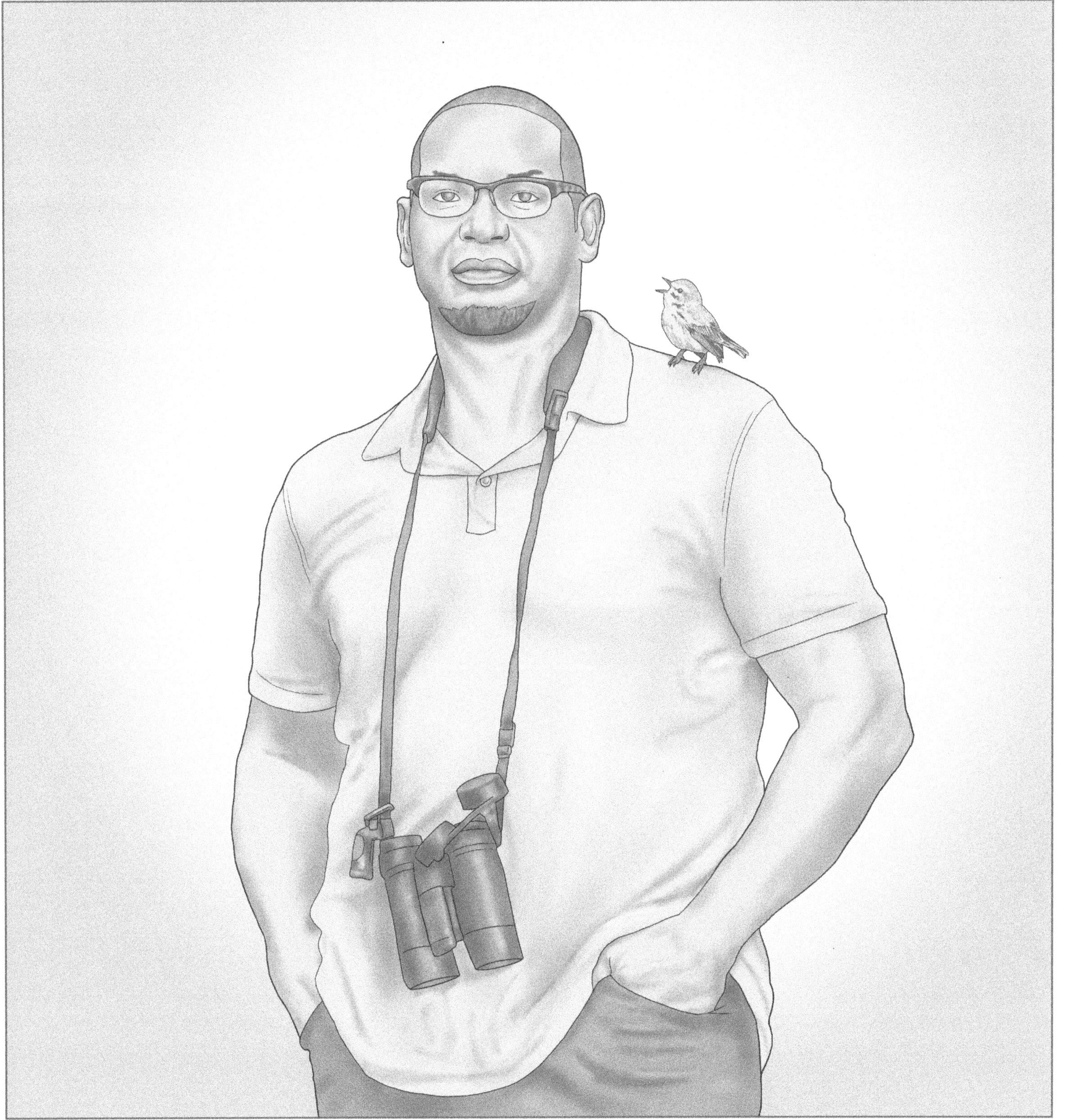

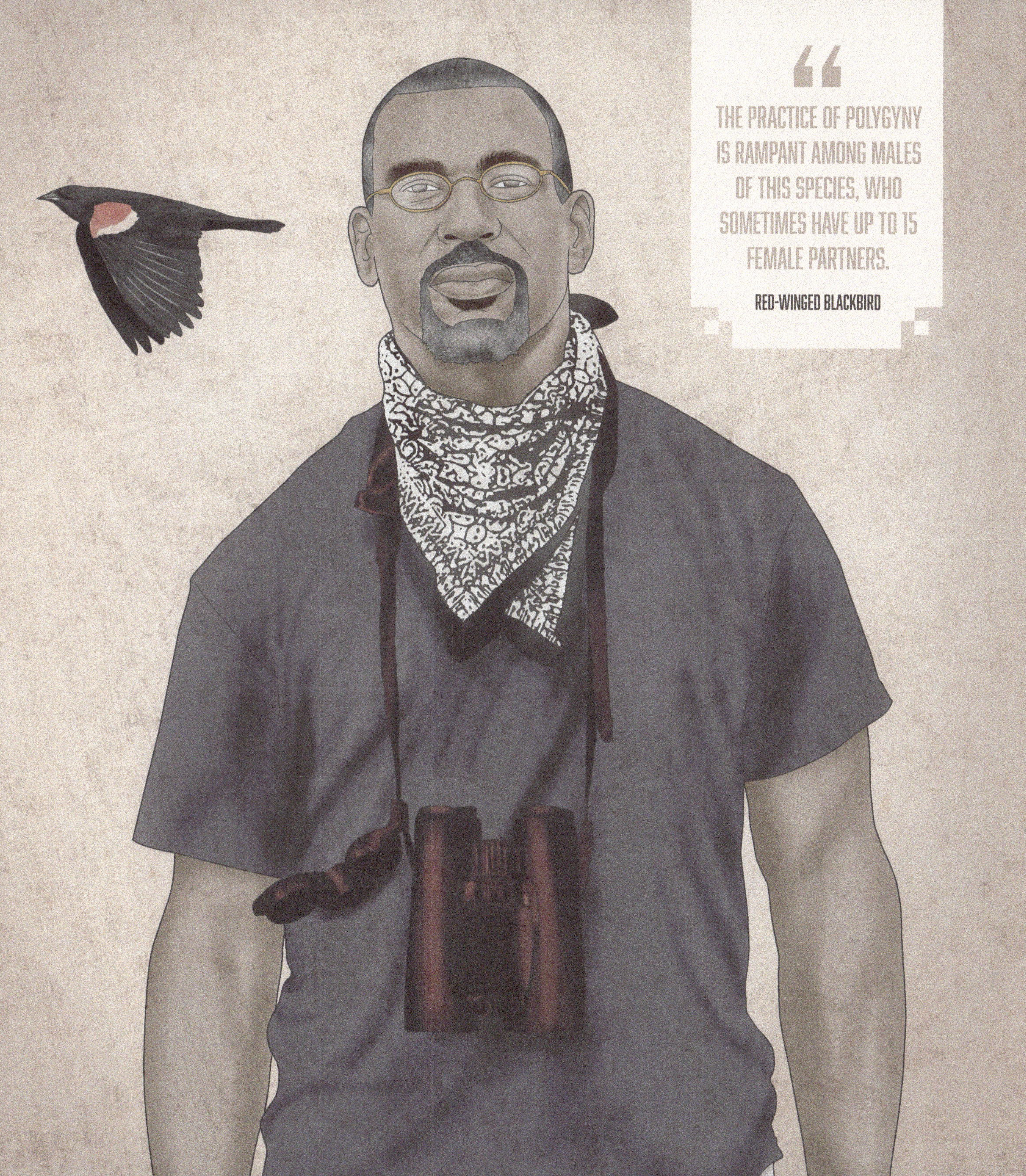

"
THE PRACTICE OF POLYGYNY IS RAMPANT AMONG MALES OF THIS SPECIES, WHO SOMETIMES HAVE UP TO 15 FEMALE PARTNERS.
RED-WINGED BLACKBIRD

CHRISTIAN COOPER

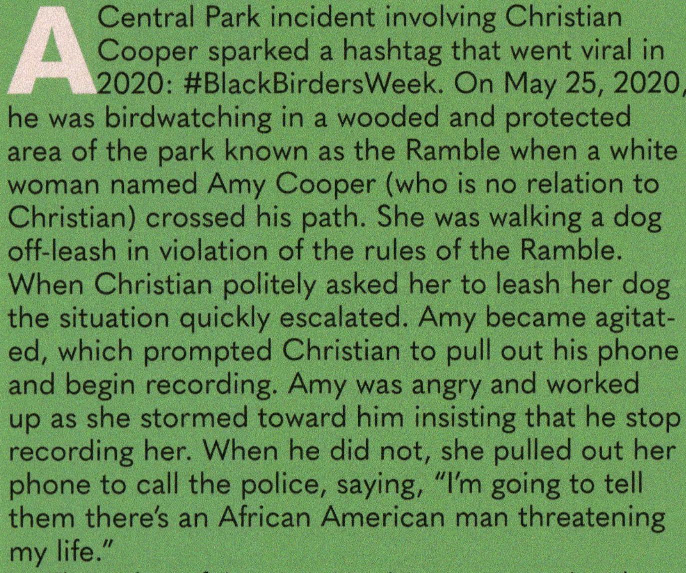

A Central Park incident involving Christian Cooper sparked a hashtag that went viral in 2020: #BlackBirdersWeek. On May 25, 2020, he was birdwatching in a wooded and protected area of the park known as the Ramble when a white woman named Amy Cooper (who is no relation to Christian) crossed his path. She was walking a dog off-leash in violation of the rules of the Ramble. When Christian politely asked her to leash her dog the situation quickly escalated. Amy became agitated, which prompted Christian to pull out his phone and begin recording. Amy was angry and worked up as she stormed toward him insisting that he stop recording her. When he did not, she pulled out her phone to call the police, saying, "I'm going to tell them there's an African American man threatening my life."

The video of Amy attempting to weaponize the police against a black birder who was within his rights has since gone viral after Christian's sister Melody posted it on Twitter. The world watched as she called the police and, speaking frantically, said that Christian was threatening her and her dog. Amy Cooper lost her job at the investment firm Franklin Templeton. The Manhattan district attorney also charged her with falsely reporting an incident in the third degree. In an opinion piece for *The Washington Post*, Christian later wrote:

> **"I think it's a mistake to focus on this one individual. The important thing the incident highlights is the long-standing, deep-seated racial bias against us black and brown folk that permeates the United States."**

He chose not to cooperate with the prosecution, which ultimately dropped the charges against Amy Cooper. But the incident led to a new state Senate bill that now criminalizes false race-based 911 calls. Governor Andrew Cuomo signed it into law in June 2020.

Christian Cooper, who was born in 1963, grew up on Long Island in New York. He keeps his personal life private for the most part, but his father was Francis Hedgeman Cooper, a science teacher and civil rights activist. Francis led a chapter of Congress of Racial Equality on Long Island. His mother taught English. Christian's love of birds began in childhood. During a cross-country trip to California, he occupied himself by reading a bird field guide. When they arrived in California, he pointed out a magpie to his parents' surprise.

Christian attended Harvard in 1980 and graduated with a bachelor's in government in 1984. During his time at Harvard, Christian joined the Harvard Ornithological Club and became its president. Christian grew up reading comics and was a big fan of Marvel superheroes. Instead of pursuing a career that was better suited to his degree, Christian applied at Marvel Comics and was hired as an associate editor. He left the company in the late 1990s and gave up on comics for a time. In May 2001, he joined Health Science Communications, an advertising agency he stayed with for close to twenty years, leaving in October 2020 as senior editorial director. **U**

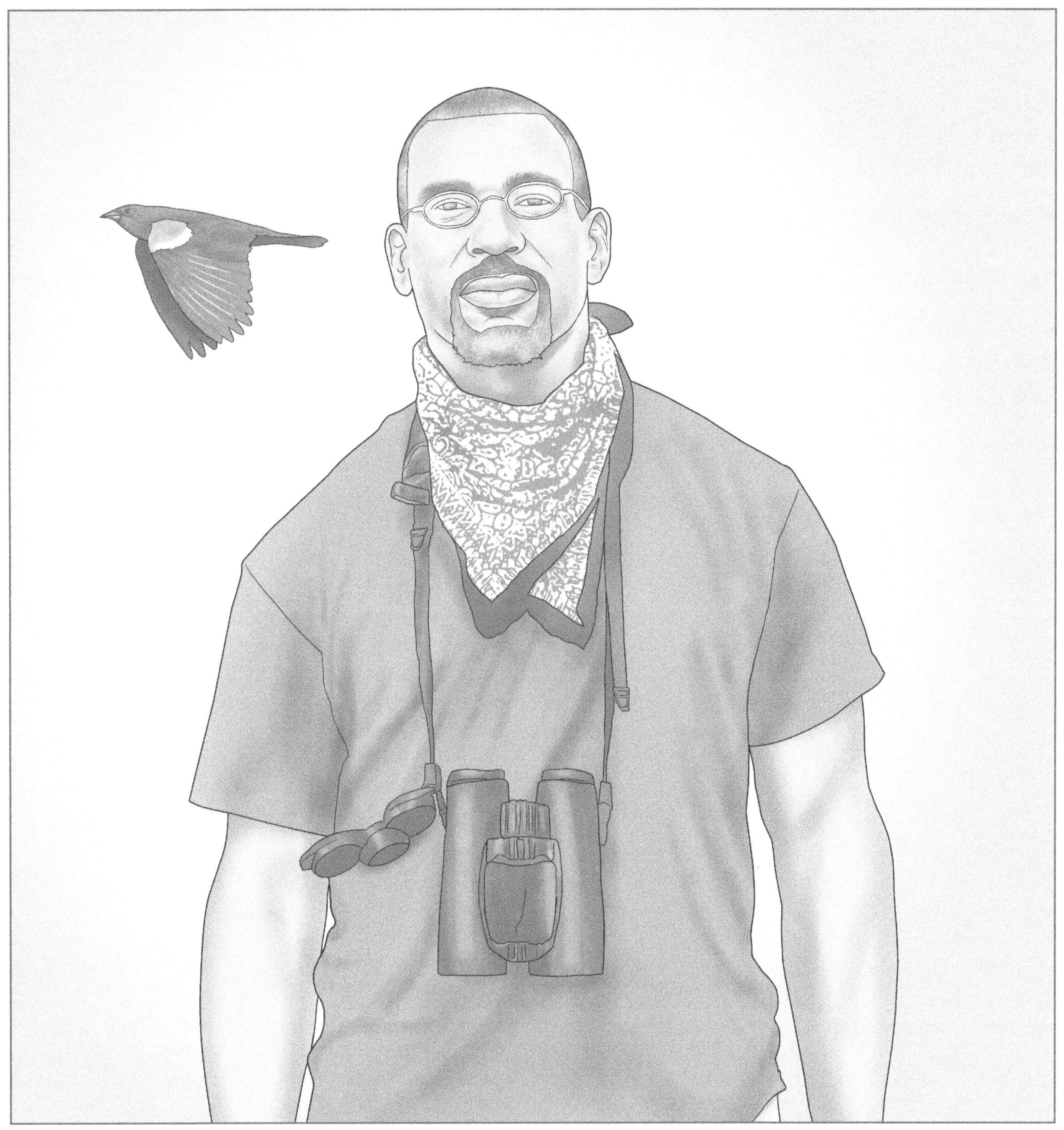

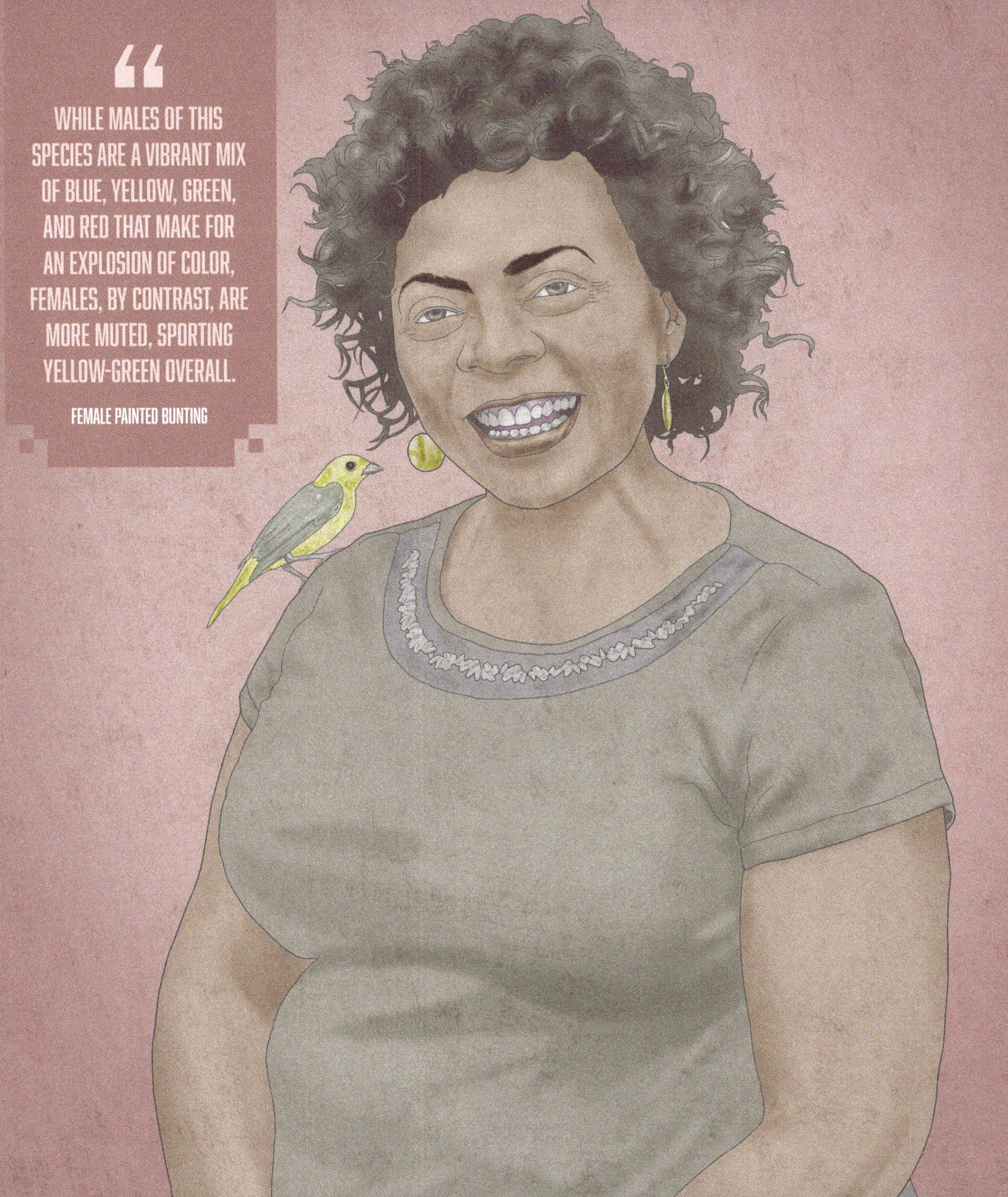
"
WHILE MALES OF THIS SPECIES ARE A VIBRANT MIX OF BLUE, YELLOW, GREEN, AND RED THAT MAKE FOR AN EXPLOSION OF COLOR, FEMALES, BY CONTRAST, ARE MORE MUTED, SPORTING YELLOW-GREEN OVERALL.

FEMALE PAINTED BUNTING

DR. MAMIE PARKER

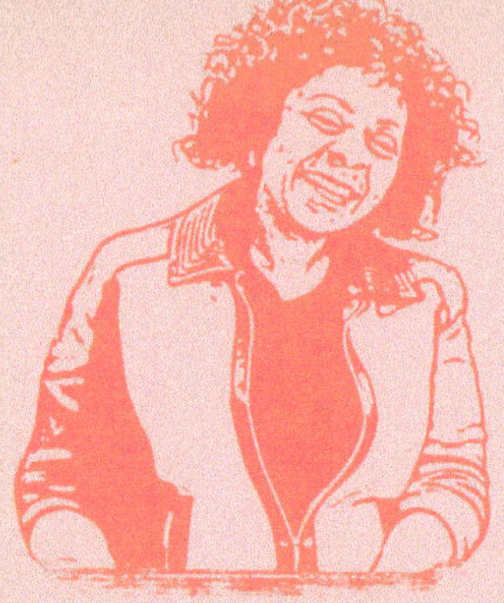

Dr. Mamie Parker, who grew up loving the outdoors through her mother's influence, became a powerhouse in wildlife conservation. She enjoyed a diverse career that saw several firsts, such as being named a U.S. Fish and Wildlife Service regional director. No black woman before her can claim that. In her role as regional director, she oversaw thirteen states in the northeast and spearheaded the removal of dams that impeded the annual migration of Atlantic salmon. Officials promoted Dr. Parker to Head of Fisheries and assistant director in the early 2000s. The Virginia Department of Wildlife Resources Board also elected Dr. Parker as its first black female chair in 2019.

Mamie Aselean Parker was born in Wilmot, Arkansas, on October 14, 1957, the youngest of 11 children. Her mother, Cora Parker, was a sharecropper who raised her children alone. Dr. Parker's mother named her after the sitting first lady of the United States, Mamie Eisenhower. Cora Parker loved fishing, and Dr. Parker developed the same love, which blossomed into a career. As a child, Dr. Parker got her introduction to fish and birds at Bayou Bartholomew, the world's longest bayou with over 360 species of fish and wildlife.

After graduating as salutatorian (or second in her class) of Wilmot High School, Dr. Parker attended the University of Arkansas at Pine Bluff (UAPB). She graduated in 1980 with a bachelor's in biology. She later attended the University of Wisconsin, earning a master's in fish and wildlife management and a PhD in microbiology. Dr. Parker began working for the USFWS in May 1977, where she remained for over four decades. In her various roles, Dr. Parker traveled the country extensively. And she was involved in conservation efforts related to national fish hatcheries, marine mammals, national wetlands, wetland restoration, and coastal mapping. In a conversation with the National Wildlife Federation, Dr. Parker stated:

> **"When I visit a protected wildlife area and know that's because of our work or our predecessors, it's exciting. I'm able to be here because someone thought this was precious enough to hold onto in this world, where everything is developing around us."**

Dr. Parker has garnered numerous awards for her work over the years. The USFWS presented her with the Ira Gabrielson Award for her outstanding leadership. She was enshrined into the Arkansas Outdoor Hall of Fame by the governor, being the first black person to receive such an induction. The University of Arkansas at Pine Bluff likewise inducted her into its hall of fame and extended its Rural Life Distinguished Leadership Award. In recognition of her outstanding leadership and role in developing the National Fish Passage Program and the National Fish Habitat Plan, President Barack Obama presented her with the Presidential Rank Award. It is the highest honor a U.S. president can bestow on government employees.

Dr. Parker retired from government in 2007, but her work in conservation never slowed. As chair of the Virginia Department of Wildlife Resources Board, she oversaw the passage of a resolution that protected migratory birds threatened by bridge construction. U

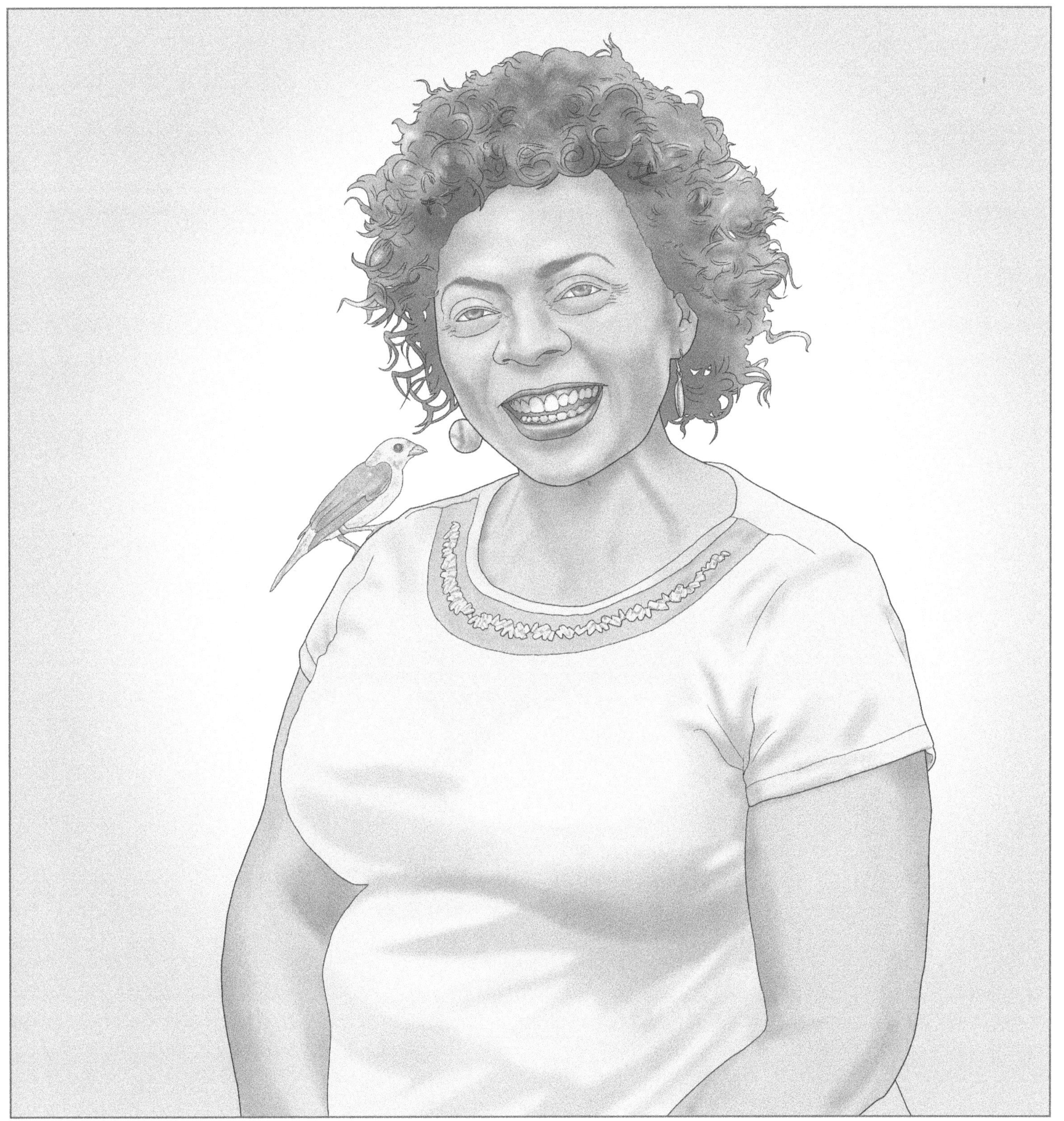

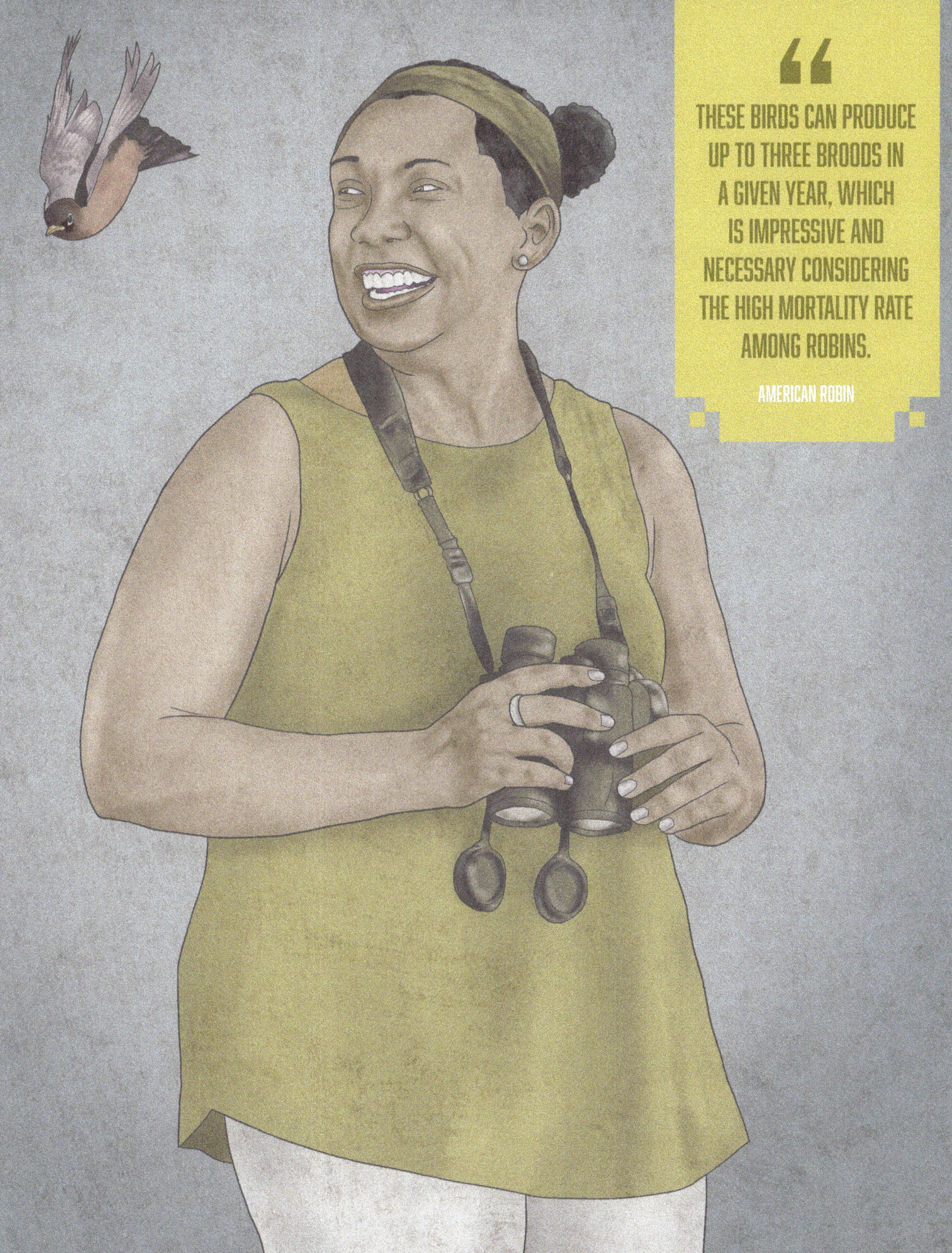
"
THESE BIRDS CAN PRODUCE
UP TO THREE BROODS IN
A GIVEN YEAR, WHICH
IS IMPRESSIVE AND
NECESSARY CONSIDERING
THE HIGH MORTALITY RATE
AMONG ROBINS.
AMERICAN ROBIN

DR. KASSANDRA FORD

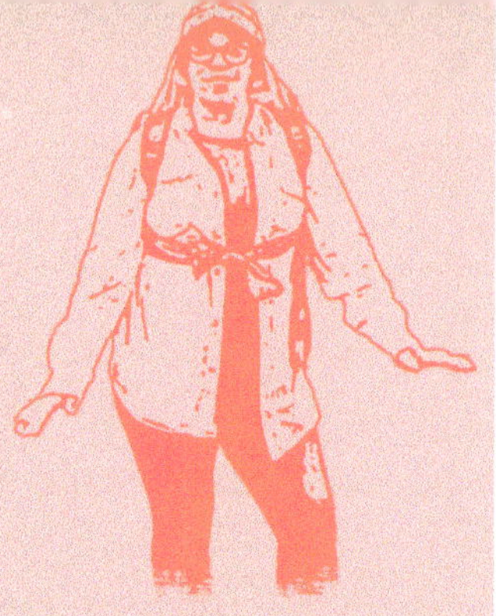

Kassandra Ford successfully defended her PhD dissertation, "Mosaic Evolution of Craniofacial Morphologies in Apteronotid and Mormyrid Weakly Electric Fishes," in summer 2021. She then flew to Switzerland to begin a short-term postdoctoral research position at the University of Bern. In April 2021, the National Science Foundation also awarded a postdoctoral research fellowship in biology, which begins in June 2022 at George Washington University.

Kassandra Ford was born in San Antonio, Texas, on March 30, 1993. Her family moved to Green Bay, Wisconsin, where she grew up. Kassandra often went camping during childhood, and she enjoyed playing outdoors. Her love of nature began with those experiences and led to her desire to enter the field of biology. But like many other aspiring black biologists of her generation, Kassandra believed the only career open to her was veterinary medicine.

She attended Martin Luther King Jr. Elementary School, Vincent T. Lombardi Middle School, and graduated from Southwest High School in 2011. While in college, she realized she could get a PhD in Biology and conduct research for a career. Kassandra spent four years at the University of Wisconsin pursuing a Bachelor of Science in Genetics as a Chancellor's Scholar. During that time, she gained three years of scientific research experience. During her undergraduate studies—which included a class that focused on animal husbandry—Kassandra realized the veterinary path was the wrong one for her. She set her sights on biological research instead.

Initially, Kassandra considered pursuing a master's degree, but her desire for a biology doctorate led her to the University of Louisiana at Lafayette. She completed her PhD in Environmental and Evolutionary Biology in 2021 under advisor Dr. James Albert. Her research focused on head and skull shape evolution in electric fishes from the tropics. Her time in Louisiana also resulted in her love of birds.

"I spent many weekends birding, hiking, and participating in bird banding. It was these interactions that introduced me to some of the other amazing black birders in the U.S."

Kassandra has since established herself as an ichthyologist (a biologist who studies all aspects of fish biology), a biomechanist (one who studies the movement in living things), and a functional morphologist (a person who studies the form and shape of organisms). Upon completing her postdoctoral research in Bern, Switzerland—where she studied the evolution of African cichlid fishes—Kassandra plans on moving to Washington, D.C., to begin her postdoctoral research position at George Washington University, which will also focus on electric fishes. Elaborating on her plans for the future, Kassandra stated:

"I plan to stay in academia and become a professor who teaches and performs research so that I can be a mentor to future students who look like me. I want those students to see someone who has been successful and done what they want to do, but who also looks like them." U

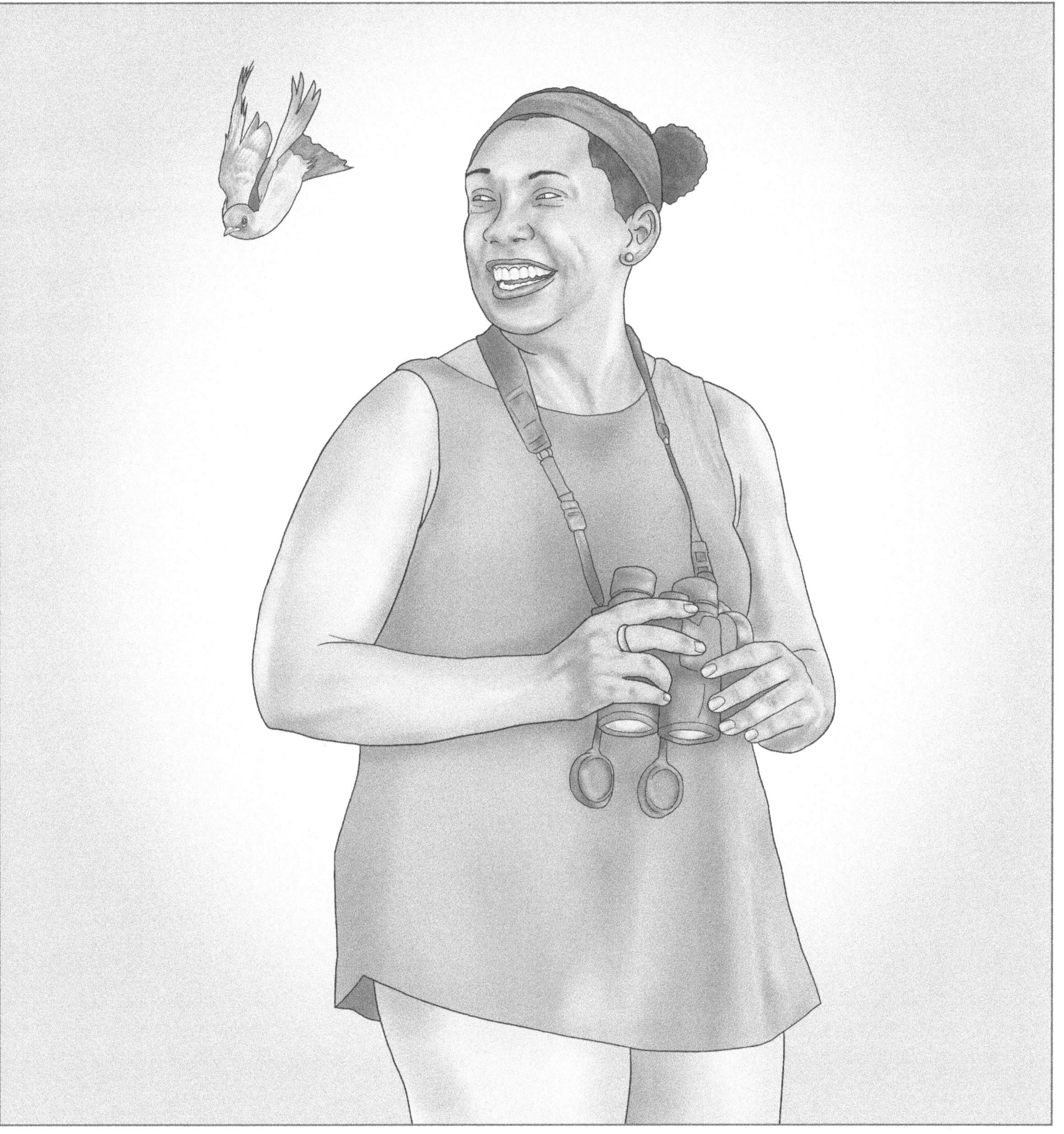

Black History
Like no other

Show your support by purchasing our title *45 People, Places & Events in Black History You Should Know.* Packed with insightful encyclopedic entries, you'll spend hours learning about hidden black history.

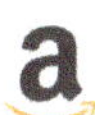
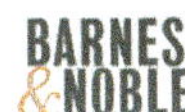
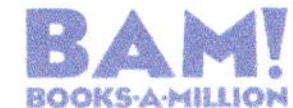

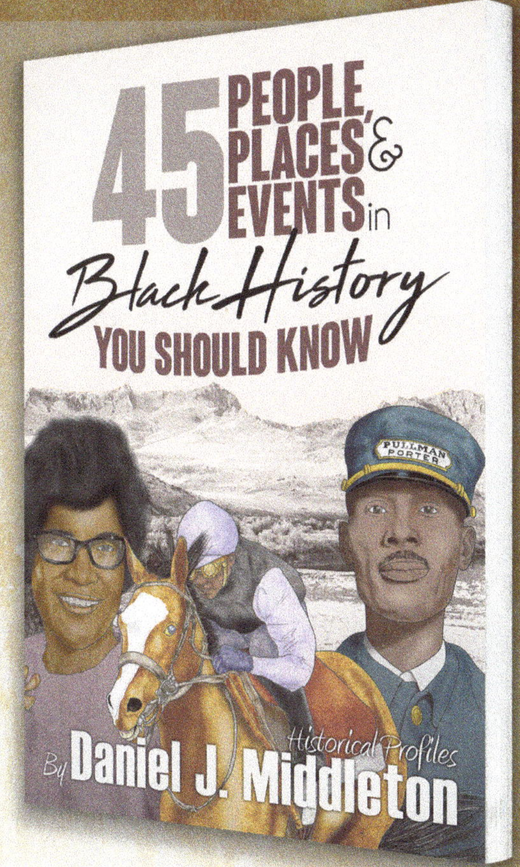

And subscribe to us on YouTube
youtube.com/uniquecoloring

Learn more by scanning the QR code using the camera on your smartphone or tablet:

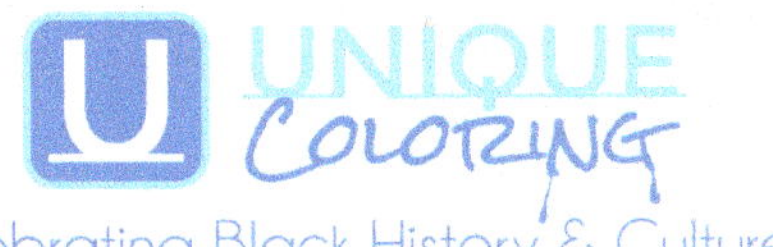

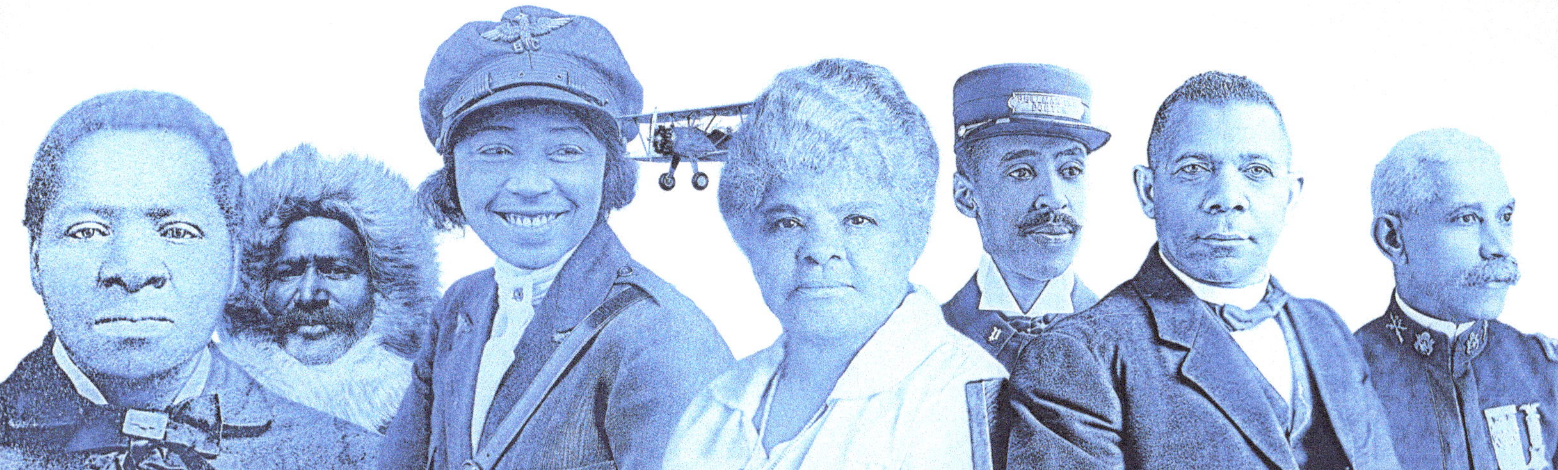

www.ingramcontent.com/pod-product-compliance
Lightning Source LLC
Chambersburg PA
CBHW042052030726

47599CB00019B/2459